ROLE OF CRYPTO IN TRANSFORMING LIVES.

Empowering People, Redefining Possibilities: The Global Impact of Cryptocurrency

DERRICK SEKIZIYIVU

Certified Digital Finance Practitioner

ROLE OF CRYPTO IN TRANSFORMING LIVES

Empowering People, Redefining Possibilities: The Global Impact of Cryptocurrency

DERRICK SEKIZIYIVU

Role of Crypto in Transforming Lives!

"Empowering People, Redefining Possibilities: The Global Impact of Cryptocurrency

Copyright Page:

Published by Therrid Publishers
Canada
www.tazzuba.com

ISBN (Paperback): 978-1-998628-30-8
ISBN (Hardcover): 978-1-998628-29-2
ISBN (Electronic Book): 978-1-998628-28-5

First Edition, 2025

For permissions or bulk orders, please contact: sekiderrick@gmail.com

Printed in Canada

Table of Contents

Dedication

To the curious minds seeking truth, the bold thinkers shaping the future, and the everyday dreamers striving for financial freedom.

This book is especially dedicated to those who have ever felt left behind by traditional systems — may you find power, possibility, and purpose in the world of crypto.

And to my family and mentors — thank you for believing in a vision before it was understood.

— Derrick Sekiziyivu

Epigraph

"The future is already here — it's just not evenly distributed."
— *William Gibson*

Foreword:

In a time when digital transformation is redefining every aspect of our lives, from communication to commerce, one of the most revolutionary changes is occurring in the way we think about money. Cryptocurrency, led by the rise of Bitcoin, has shifted from being a fringe concept to a mainstream movement—both a technological breakthrough and a financial awakening.

Yet for many, the world of crypto remains shrouded in complexity and confusion. What is Bitcoin? How does it work? Is it safe, legal, or even necessary? These are just a few of the pressing questions that millions are asking as they stand at the edge of this rapidly evolving frontier.

That's where *Crypto Unlocked* comes in. With clarity, depth, and approachability, Derrick Sekiziyivu—a Certified Digital Finance Practitioner—breaks down the barriers to understanding cryptocurrency. Drawing from years of research, personal insights, and practical experience, Derrick offers more than just explanations—he provides answers.

This book is for the curious and the cautious. For those who've heard the buzzwords—blockchain, DeFi, NFTs—but haven't yet seen the bigger picture. It's for those looking to take their first step into the crypto space, and for others who want to deepen their knowledge with confidence.

What makes this book special is not just the content—it's the heart behind it. Derrick believes in the transformative power of crypto to empower individuals, democratize finance, and spark global inclusion. His voice is calm, wise, and grounded—not a hype machine, but a reliable guide through a noisy and often overwhelming space.

As you turn these pages, I invite you to lean into the questions, reflect on the possibilities, and imagine a future where financial empowerment is not the privilege of a few, but the right of all.

Welcome to the new frontier. Let's unlock it—together.

Preface

When I first encountered Bitcoin, I was both intrigued and skeptical. The idea of digital money—borderless, decentralized, and cryptographically secure—felt more like science fiction than financial evolution. But as I dug deeper, what I discovered wasn't just a new kind of currency; it was the beginning of a global shift.

This book was born out of the countless questions I've heard from friends, professionals, students, and even financial experts: *Is Bitcoin safe? Who controls it? Can I trust it? How does it work? Is this just a passing trend?*

I realized then that what people needed wasn't more technical jargon or hype-filled speculation—they needed clarity, truth, and simplicity. They needed a guide that could answer their most important questions without condescension or confusion.

Crypto Unlocked is that guide. It's for the beginner and the curious, for the cautious investor and the hopeful innovator. Whether you've never bought crypto or you're looking to deepen your understanding of its purpose and potential, this book is here to inform and empower you.

You'll find explanations, practical insights, and reflections grounded in my work as a Certified Digital Finance Practitioner. But more than that, you'll find a deep belief in the transformative power of cryptocurrency—not just as a financial tool, but as a vehicle for global change.

We are living through a financial revolution. This book is your invitation to join it—equipped, confident, and ready to unlock the future of money.

Derrick Sekiziyivu
Certified Digital Finance Practitioner

Acknowledgments

This book is the result of the support, inspiration, and collaboration of many remarkable individuals and communities.

First, I am deeply grateful to my family for their unwavering encouragement, patience, and belief in my vision. Your love has been my anchor throughout this journey.

To the early adopters, innovators, and everyday people around the world who shared their stories of how cryptocurrency has touched their lives—thank you for your openness and honesty. Your experiences are the heartbeat of this book.

Special thanks to my colleagues and friends in the blockchain and fintech communities, whose insights, debates, and feedback challenged me to think deeper and reach higher. Your passion for positive change is contagious.

I am also indebted to the educators, researchers, and thought leaders who have tirelessly worked to make cryptocurrency accessible and understandable for all. Your commitment to spreading knowledge is building a more inclusive financial future.

To the team at Therrid Publishers—thank you for your professionalism, creativity, and dedication to excellence. Your support brought this project from idea to reality.

Finally, to every reader who believes in the power of transformation—financial, personal, and societal—through knowledge and innovation: this book is for you.

With heartfelt appreciation,

Derrick Sekiziyivu

Introduction:
Role of Crypto in Transforming Lives

"Empowering People, Redefining Possibilities: The Global Impact of Cryptocurrency"

From the bustling cities of financial innovation to remote communities long excluded from traditional banking, cryptocurrency is doing more than reshaping economies—it's transforming lives. This book is a reflection of that transformation.

For **Derrick Sekiziyivu**, a Certified Digital Finance Practitioner, the crypto journey is deeply personal. Witnessing the systemic limitations of conventional finance, especially across emerging markets, Derrick was driven to explore the liberating potential of decentralized finance.

In a world where the future of money is being reimagined in real time, he knew the moment to speak was now.

Why this book?
Because there are still too many unanswered questions. Too many myths. And too many people unsure of where to begin.

Why now?
Because we stand on the edge of a revolution. And understanding crypto isn't just about finance—it's about freedom, access, empowerment, and rewriting what's possible for the future of humanity.

Whether you're curious, skeptical, or ready to dive in—this book is your guide to the answers you've been seeking.

In the ever-evolving landscape of technology and finance, one remarkable journey stands out as a beacon of curiosity and innovation. Derrick's story is not just about personal exploration but serves as an illuminating guidepost for anyone stepping into the world of cryptocurrency. As we witness the rapid transformation from obscure technological experiment to a globally recognized financial movement, it's more important than ever to explore why this book, and why now.
Derrick was first introduced to cryptocurrency during a casual conversation at a coffee shop, when a friend excitedly mentioned Bitcoin. Like many of you, he was intrigued yet overwhelmed by the technical jargon and complex concepts surrounding digital currencies. Why were people so passionate? How could something that's completely virtual hold such promise and potential? Driven by these questions, Derrick embarked on a journey to understand what cryptocurrency truly meant—not just for tech enthusiasts or financial mavens, but for everyone. This book is the culmination of that journey—a path filled with learning, exploration, and the realization of the profound impact crypto is having across the globe.

The rise of cryptocurrency has been nothing short of meteoric. What started as a niche technological innovation—one born out of the ashes of the 2008 financial crisis—has grown into a global phenomenon. At its core, cryptocurrency challenges our traditional notions of money, spearheading a movement towards decentralized financial systems that give individuals control over their own wealth. This shift from centralized authority to individual empowerment is reshaping economies, industries, and even government policies worldwide. It's a movement that's hard to ignore, whether you're a curious newcomer, a budding investor, or a seasoned professional.

Yet, for many, the complex terminology and the seemingly opaque nature of blockchain technology can be daunting. That's where this book comes in. Our aim is to cut through the noise and present a clear, trustworthy overview of how crypto is impacting lives across continents. By focusing on relatable stories and real-world applications, we hope to demystify the technology and bring clarity to your questions—whether it's understanding the basics of buying and storing Bitcoin safely, or delving into the transformative power of decentralized finance.

For those who are new to crypto, think of this book as an accessible portal to a fascinating frontier. Here, you'll find straightforward answers to common questions, helping bridge the gap between curiosity and knowledge. Aspiring and early investors will appreciate our detailed insights into getting started with digital assets, providing the confidence needed to make informed decisions. You'll learn about key concepts like wallets, exchanges, and security measures—essentials for safeguarding your investments.

Professionals and entrepreneurs, this book invites you to consider the integration of crypto into your business practices. Whether you're in fintech, banking, or simply looking to accept crypto payments, we'll empower you with foundational knowledge to navigate this dynamic landscape. For students and educators, we've crafted explanations that introduce blockchain and crypto topics with clarity, fostering a deeper understanding of modern finance.

But the reach of cryptocurrency extends even further. Policymakers and development practitioners stand to gain insights into how crypto could revolutionize financial inclusion efforts, streamline remittances, and drive economic empowerment. Imagine a world were sending money abroad is fast, affordable, and without intermediaries. Consider the potential for decentralized finance to create opportunities in emerging markets previously excluded from traditional banking systems.

As you delve into the pages ahead, you'll discover how crypto is more than a speculative asset or a fleeting trend. It's a powerful tool with the capacity to redefine industries and empower individuals at every corner of the globe. The narratives we'll share underscore the real-life impacts of crypto—from farmers in Africa accessing new markets, to small businesses leveraging Bitcoin for growth, to students worldwide embracing financial literacy through blockchain education.

This book seeks to break down barriers by using straightforward, modern language and maintaining a conversational tone throughout. We want you to feel like you're engaging in a dialogue rather than deciphering a technical manual. Our authoritative approach ensures you receive accurate, reliable information, supporting your journey with context and clarity.

Ultimately, Derrick's story mirrors the broader cultural and economic shifts we're witnessing today. Cryptocurrency is no longer confined to underground circles; it's a force driving tangible change and innovation. Whether you're here out of curiosity or intent on exploring investment opportunities, this book offers a roadmap tailored for today's multifaceted audience.

So, join us on this journey of discovery and empowerment. Together, let's unpack the complex, exhilarating world of cryptocurrency. Welcome to a movement that's redefining the way we think about money, trust, and the potential of human ingenuity. Welcome to the next chapter in financial history. Welcome to the exploration of possibilities unleashed by crypto.

Chapter 1: *What is Cryptocurrency?*

Understanding Cryptocurrency

Have you ever wondered why digital money is becoming the talk of modern finance, or why people are investing in something they can't hold in their hands? The concept of cryptocurrency has intrigued many with its promises of decentralization and financial freedom. How does cryptography ensure that these currencies remain secure, and what makes them different from the cash we use every day? These questions might cross your mind as you hear buzzwords like "blockchain" and "Bitcoin" swirling around conversations about the future of money.

In this chapter, we're diving into the world of cryptocurrency to answer these inquiries and more. You'll gain a clear understanding of this digital currency, exploring its origins and the core technologies that give it strength. From the revolutionary idea behind blockchain to how cryptocurrencies operate without middlemen, we'll provide a comprehensive overview that lays the foundation for grasping their significance in reshaping our global financial landscape. Whether you're new to this topic or seeking deeper insights, you'll soon discover why cryptocurrencies are capturing the world's attention.

Introduction to Cryptocurrency

Cryptocurrency is a form of currency that exists entirely in digital or virtual form. Unlike physical money, cryptocurrency does not have a tangible form like coins or banknotes. Instead, it resides in digital wallets online. But what truly sets it apart from traditional money is the way it ensures security and trust: through cryptography.

Cryptography is the practice of securing information by transforming it into a format that can only be understood by someone who possesses special knowledge, usually referred to as a cryptographic key. This technology ensures that transactions conducted with cryptocurrencies remain confidential and secure. When you send Bitcoin or any other cryptocurrency, cryptography protects the data by encrypting it. Thus, even if someone intercepts this data, they cannot decipher it without the appropriate key. This feature of security is a major reason why cryptocurrencies have gained popularity.

But cryptography alone doesn't tell the full story of why cryptocurrencies are considered revolutionary. Another fundamental aspect is decentralization. Unlike traditional currencies, which are regulated by central banks and governments, cryptocurrencies operate on a decentralized network. This means no single entity owns, controls, or can manipulate the currency. Instead, a network of computers, often referred to as nodes, runs the blockchain that supports these currencies.

And what exactly is a blockchain? At its heart, blockchain is a public ledger that records all transactions across a network of computers. This ledger is accessible to anyone and cannot be altered without consensus from the network. Every transaction made with cryptocurrency is permanently recorded on the blockchain and is visible to everyone in the network. This transparency builds trust among users because they can view and verify all transactions independently.

Imagine a notebook that everyone can see, but once you write something in it, you can't erase it. That's essentially what the blockchain does. It prevents fraud, double-spending, and ensures that the currency isn't counterfeited. Each block in the blockchain holds several transactions, and when a block is completed, it gets added to the chain. This continuous and secure method of recording information ensures that the system remains tamper-proof.

This idea of a decentralized network eliminates the middleman, which is quintessential in traditional financial transactions. When we transfer money via banks, those banks act as intermediaries. With cryptocurrency, the peer-to-peer network allows individuals to transact directly without a middle party. This aspect not only places control back in the hands of users but also reduces transaction costs.

Let's say you want to send money to a friend who lives across the world. Using traditional banks, you may encounter high fees and delays, especially on weekends or holidays. Cryptocurrencies operate 24/7, and the fees are often significantly lower. This accessibility and cost-effectiveness are highly appealing to its users.

Bitcoin, the first and most renowned cryptocurrency, was created specifically to provide an alternative financial system, one that isn't bound by borders or governed by centralized institutions. Since its inception in 2009, Bitcoin has spurred the development of thousands of other cryptocurrencies, each designed with specific purposes in mind. For example, Ethereum offers smart contracts, enabling developers to build decentralized applications (DApps).

As people begin to understand and explore these decentralized financial alternatives, they see the potential for reshaping the global economy. Cryptocurrencies open avenues for financial inclusion, allowing those without access to traditional banking to engage in the global economy. All one needs is a smartphone and an internet connection to start using cryptocurrency, making it an attractive option for the underbanked populations.

To provide a concrete example, consider cross-border remittances. Many individuals work in foreign countries and remit money to their families back home. Traditional remittance services like Western Union or MoneyGram can be expensive and time-consuming. But cryptocurrency transactions allow for fast, low-cost transfers directly from sender to recipient, streamlining the process and reducing reliance on costly intermediaries.

This accessibility extends beyond individuals to businesses as well. Small and medium enterprises, particularly in developing countries, can benefit from reduced transaction fees and enhanced access to international markets. Companies can offer their services to a broader audience without being constrained by the traditional banking system.

Though cryptocurrencies present significant potential, they also face challenges. Volatility remains one of the most significant hurdles. Prices can fluctuate wildly in short timeframes, which can be daunting for new users. Regulatory uncertainty also poses a challenge. Different countries approach cryptocurrency legislation differently, leading to a patchwork of regulations worldwide. While some embrace it, others restrict or even ban its use.

The journey of digital currency didn't start with Bitcoin. Its origins trace back to several early digital cash projects from the late 20th century. One such project was Digicash, introduced in the 1980s, which aimed to create anonymous electronic money. Though it eventually failed due to several factors, Digicash laid foundational ideas for what would become modern cryptocurrencies. It highlighted the potential of digital money to foster

anonymous and secure transactions, concepts that later influenced Bitcoin's creation and success.
With this understanding of core concepts like digital currency, cryptography, decentralization, and blockchain, it's crucial to see how they intersect to form the backbone of cryptocurrency's appeal. As we look further into the historical trajectory of digital currencies and their evolution, we'll explore how these early projects influenced the architecture of today's cryptocurrency landscape and sparked an era of financial innovation.

Origins of Digital Money

Continuing from where we left off with an understanding of cryptocurrency as digital currency secured by cryptography and utilizing decentralized technology, let's delve into the evolution of digital money that set the stage for the cryptocurrencies we know today. It's fascinating to trace the roots of digital currency back to the late 20th century. During this time, there was a burgeoning interest in creating electronic forms of cash. One of the earliest projects, Digicash, started in the late 1980s, was pioneering in its attempt to digitize money. Conceived by David Chaum, Digicash aimed to create a currency that could be transferred electronically with the promise of privacy and security through cryptographic techniques. This concept was revolutionary at the time, laying down the principles of electronic cash and cryptographic security, which are now foundational to cryptocurrencies.
Despite its eventual downfall due to market conditions and technological limitations, Digicash was instrumental in setting the stage for future developments. The focus on security and privacy drove further innovations and led to the emergence of other digital money projects. Throughout the 1990s, enthusiasm grew around the possibilities of digital transactions and the potential efficiencies they could bring to traditional financial systems. Companies began to experiment with creating digital currencies that promised to make money transfers more seamless, efficient, and less costly.

Alongside Digicash, B-money and Bit Gold emerged as notable efforts in the evolution of digital money. B-money, proposed by Wei Dai, introduced the concept of using cryptographic formulas to facilitate the creation and exchange of currency without central authority—a fundamental principle that would later define cryptocurrencies. Though it never came into practical use, B-money's vision inspired later innovations. Similarly, Bit Gold, conceptualized by Nick Szabo, shared similar cryptographic foundations and ideas about a decentralized money system. These early projects, while not evolving into full-fledged digital currencies, helped solidify concepts such as the blockchain and decentralized systems, which would become critical elements in the structure of cryptocurrencies.
Let's consider how these innovations affected the trajectory of digital financial systems. The transition from these initial concepts to cryptocurrencies involved several critical advancements. Firstly, the advancement of cryptographic techniques provided a robust security framework, essential for protecting digital transactions. The concept of public and private keys, for instance, became a cornerstone for ensuring that transactions were kept confidential and tamper-proof. This cryptographic security became a silver bullet in addressing trust issues with digital transactions, a long-standing barrier to the acceptance and proliferation of digital money.

Additionally, the idea of decentralized control was key in moving away from traditional financial systems that relied heavily on central authorities like banks and governments. By distributing control across a network, digital currency could reduce vulnerabilities associated with single points of failure, making the system more resilient to attacks and manipulation. This shift started rendering traditional financial systems less suitable for the emerging digital economy. The seeds planted by Digicash, B-money, and Bit Gold demonstrated the possibility of a parallel financial system built on digital trust, which resonated with technologists and finance enthusiasts navigating a rapidly digitizing world.

Fast-forward to 2009, and we see the introduction of Bitcoin, a significant leap forward in the evolution from early digital money concepts to a fully functioning cryptocurrency. Bitcoin wasn't just a digital currency; it was a complete overhaul of how financial transactions could be managed, verified, and trusted. By successfully implementing the blockchain—a public ledger that records transactions across multiple computers—Bitcoin exemplified how technical concepts introduced decades earlier could effectively operate at scale. It showed how digital money could exist independently of traditional banking systems, functioning securely within a decentralized network.

In practical terms, Bitcoin demonstrated the real-world application of blockchain technology, which captured the public's imagination and interest. The rapid adoption of Bitcoin showcased how the foundational work of early digital money pioneers could be integrated into a cohesive system with real-world utility. The core principles of security, decentralization, and privacy, first explored in the 1990s, had come to fruition in a mainstream technology that could be used by anyone with internet access.

This explosion of interest in Bitcoin paved the way for further developments in the realm of digital currencies. By 2015, Ethereum took an important next step by using blockchain technology to create a platform that allowed for more than just simple transactions. Ethereum introduced smart contracts—self-executing contracts with the terms of agreement directly written into code. This innovation marked a pivotal expansion in blockchain applications, demonstrating its potential beyond currency. Smart contracts automated traditional processes and introduced possibilities for complex, programmable interactions on the blockchain.

Ethereum's introduction drove home the point that blockchain technology could be a platform for variety beyond digital currencies. It indicated a future where blockchain and cryptocurrencies could reshape industries by improving efficiencies, reducing costs, and driving innovation. These forward-looking ideas have rallied enthusiasts globally, who continue to develop blockchain-based solutions for problems across sectors, from finance and supply chain management to health care and voting systems.

In the context of this evolutionary journey, the role of foundational digital money principles becomes evident—it laid down the tracks for a financial revolution. This chapter serves to connect these dots, from early innovations like Digicash to trailblazers like Bitcoin and Ethereum. The transition from theory to successful implementation signifies that the future of cryptocurrencies holds vast potential. It suggests that the technological transformation initiated by Bitcoin in 2009 will continue to evolve, carrying forward principles ingrained by its predecessors.

As we move into the next section, we'll explore how these technologies have spurred substantial growth since the advent of Bitcoin, and how they are shaping the world today. Ethereum's smart contracts and the versatile application of blockchain indicate that we've only scratched the surface of what these technologies can do. We will examine their increasing impact on global finance, the diversification of blockchain applications, and how emerging innovations challenge our conventional understanding of financial systems.

Evolution of Cryptocurrency

The history of digital money provides a fascinating backdrop as we transition to Bitcoin's introduction in 2009. Early forms such as Digicash set the stage by attempting to address privacy and decentralization concerns, yet failed to gain traction due to various technological and market limitations. Thus, Bitcoin emerged as a revolutionary force offering decentralization and security through its groundbreaking use of blockchain technology. Its introduction marked the dawn of a new era, one in which financial transactions could occur without intermediaries. Bitcoin tackled the double-spending problem that plagued prior digital money experiments, introducing a peer-to-peer network that maintained a secure and transparent ledger of all transactions.

Since Bitcoin, cryptocurrencies have undergone a remarkable transformation, with key milestones shaping their trajectory. One pivotal development was the advent of smart contracts, popularized by the Ethereum platform in 2015. While Bitcoin primarily functions as digital gold or a store of value, Ethereum expanded the potential of blockchain technology beyond currency. Smart contracts are self-executing agreements where the terms are directly written into code. These contracts run on Ethereum's blockchain, allowing for automation and reducing the need for traditional intermediaries like banks or lawyers.

The introduction of Ethereum and its smart contracts opened up endless possibilities and spurred the growth of decentralized applications (dApps). For beginners and aspiring investors, the implications of these advancements mean an opportunity to explore and participate in areas beyond simple transactions, such as decentralized finance (DeFi). DeFi uses blockchain technology to recreate traditional financial services like lending, borrowing, and trading without central authority.

Cryptocurrencies have gradually embedded themselves into the fabric of traditional financial systems. For business professionals, especially within financial sectors, understanding this evolving ecosystem presents both challenges and opportunities. One practical example of blockchain's impact is seen in supply chain management, where smart contracts can automate and validate transactions between manufacturers and suppliers, ensuring transparency and efficiency.

Educators are witnessing these technological developments spillover into curricula. By incorporating blockchain and cryptocurrency courses, educational institutions are preparing students for an economy increasingly driven by digital assets. Courses can provide a foundation in blockchain technology, digital currencies, and their potential applications, thus equipping students with the knowledge needed for careers in diverse fields beyond just finance, such as programming or cybersecurity.

Policy makers, however, face distinct challenges. The decentralized nature of blockchain technology raises questions about regulation, taxation, and consumer protection. It's crucial for these stakeholders to strike a balance between fostering innovation and safeguarding economic stability and security. For example, knowing how to regulate Initial Coin Offerings (ICOs), which are a new form of capital raising using cryptocurrencies, requires an understanding of both the risks and potential economic

benefits involved.
The explosion of interest and investment in cryptocurrencies like Ethereum and Bitcoin exemplifies their disruptive potential and importance across various industries. Major corporations such as Tesla and Square have taken positions in Bitcoin. Meanwhile, the integration of cryptocurrencies into everyday life continues, with platforms like PayPal facilitating their use in transactions.
Some skeptics highlight volatility as a significant concern. While it's true that cryptocurrencies have experienced extreme price swings, the growing institutional interest and application within financial systems cannot be ignored. For example, El Salvador's adoption of Bitcoin as legal tender showcases a government embracing digital currency on a national scale, although it also brings questions about implementation and economic impacts.

The journey from early digital money to the sophisticated ecosystem of cryptocurrencies shows how foundational technologies like Bitcoin and Ethereum lay the groundwork for an expansive and varied set of applications. They have ignited a shift towards decentralization by empowering individuals and providing alternatives to traditional finance. Cryptocurrency projects today continue to push boundaries and explore new terrains, from non-fungible tokens (NFTs) in digital art to blockchain applications in privacy and identity verification.
Before continuing to blockchain itself, understanding the way these innovations interlink paints a clearer picture of the broader cryptocurrency landscape. The decentralized promise of blockchain underpins the security, transparency, and efficiency that make cryptocurrencies appealing. Blockchain's role as the essential technology behind Bitcoin and Ethereum holds immense value and significance. As the foundation upon which these digital currencies rest, blockchain technology ensures the integrity and immutability of ledgers, creating trust in an otherwise trustless environment.
Grasping the concept of blockchain is paramount for anyone looking to fully comprehend the full utility and potential of cryptocurrencies. As we delve further, seeing how blockchain technology affects sectors, future applications, and its emerging impact on the global economy becomes not just relevant but necessary for stakeholders at every level of engagement.

Key Concept: *Blockchain*
The growth of cryptocurrency since Bitcoin's introduction in 2009 serves as a fascinating tale of innovation and exploration. Bitcoin paved the way for a new financial landscape, opening doors to concepts such as Ethereum and smart contracts. These developments broadened the horizon beyond simple currency transactions, suggesting possibilities far-reaching and transformative. This evolution leads us into the heart of the mechanism that makes cryptocurrency what it is—blockchain technology.
At its core, blockchain technology underpins all cryptocurrencies, acting as the foundation upon which this digital revolution is built. Think of blockchain as a distributed ledger, not contained by any single entity but instead shared among participants. This structure inherently provides security and transparency, rebalancing trust in financial transactions without relying on central authorities, like banks or governments.
Imagine you are part of a group of friends, and you all share access to a digital notebook. Each entry in this notebook represents a transaction, and every friend has a copy. If one tries to alter a previous entry, the others quickly notice the discrepancy. That's

blockchain in action—ensuring data integrity with transparency. Every participant can see the transactions, which are unchangeable once recorded. This prevents foul play or fraud, as any tampering attempts are immediately evident.

Beyond securing financial exchanges, this technology finds practical applications in various industries. Consider supply chain management, where each step, from production to delivery, can be documented on a blockchain. This transparency ensures authenticity and quality, allowing consumers to verify the origins of their products. Or take digital identity verification, where blockchain offers secure and tamper-proof personal data storage, reducing identity theft.

Furthermore, blockchain eliminates the need for intermediaries by facilitating direct transactions between parties. This removes layers of bureaucratic oversight and reduces costs, which is particularly advantageous in international trade. By cutting out middlemen, blockchain streamlines processes, making them more efficient and less prone to errors.

One might wonder how all this is achieved without someone overseeing the system. The answer lies in the decentralized nature of blockchain. The network's participants collaboratively validate transactions, governed by consensus protocols. Imagine a group voting system where decisions are made collectively, ensuring agreement before any transaction is approved. This system not only assures security but also enhances fairness, as control doesn't rest in the hands of a single power.

Cryptocurrencies operate on this principle of decentralization. Bitcoin, the pioneer, demonstrated how trust can be maintained without central banks. Ethereum added another layer with its smart contracts—self-executing agreements coded directly on the blockchain, eliminating the need for external validation systems. For instance, imagine a vending machine for digital assets: you input requirements, and once conditions are met, the item is automatically dispensed. Smart contracts operate similarly, automating transactions based on pre-set conditions.

With these tools, blockchain becomes a platform for innovation. Developers can build applications that leverage this secure and open framework for uses beyond what was initially imagined. Decentralized applications, or dApps, run on blockchain networks, offering services ranging from financial tools to social networks. Each dApp operates independently, without centralized control, capitalizing on blockchain's strengths in security and transparency.

To ensure clarity and avoid redundancy now brings focus to differentiating between various blockchain applications. Within supply chains, digitizing each transaction step offers unprecedented transparency, enabling stakeholders to trace products back to their origins. It becomes easier to validate production standards, ensuring quality. Meanwhile, digital identity systems leveraging blockchain decrease vulnerability by storing personal information securely, replacing scattered databases prone to breaches.

The ability to witness and verify transactions in real-time changes how businesses operate. From reducing paperwork to accelerating transaction speed, blockchain optimization of resource allocation allows for more agile business strategies. Think of it as moving from a traditional postal system to instantaneous email communication. Transactions occur in real-time, empowering businesses with newfound efficiency.

As businesses utilize blockchain, cost reductions from cutting out intermediaries turn resources towards innovation and growth. The automotive industry, for example, might see enhanced systems for part verification and certification, diminishing counterfeit parts and ensuring safety and quality. In essence, blockchain's transparency and efficiency unlock opportunities to refine processes across sectors, enhancing reliability and trust.

Transitioning now to what lies beyond the foundational blockchain is the concept of decentralization, pivotal in empowering individuals and reshaping industries. Decentralization removes intermediaries, providing autonomy and control directly to users. Through decentralized networks, data ownership shifts, redefining how assets are shared and controlled.

Tokens play a crucial role, representing assets or utilities on a blockchain. They symbolize ownership in digital and real-world assets, aligning with the decentralized narrative by enabling peer-to-peer exchanges. Understanding the significance of tokens and their applications sets the stage for exploring how decentralization unfolds in diverse realms ahead.

Cryptocurrencies, thus, are more than just digital money; they symbolize a shift in how we conceive and manage trust, assets, and technology. The next section will dive deeper into these aspects, expanding on how decentralization and tokens form the bedrock for an innovative future.

Key Concepts: *Decentralization and Tokens*

As we explored in the previous section, blockchain technology stands as the backbone of cryptocurrencies, offering transparency and security that few other systems can match. It's this very technology that anchors the concept of decentralization. When we talk about decentralization in the context of cryptocurrencies, we're referring to the ability to operate without the need for central authorities like traditional banks or governing entities. The power of decentralized financial systems lies in their ability to eliminate intermediaries altogether, placing control—in theory—back into the hands of individuals and the community at large.

Decentralization fundamentally changes how we think about money and value transfer. One of the most striking features of decentralized cryptocurrencies is the disintermediation they offer. This essentially means that transactions can occur directly between parties without needing a trusted third-party intermediary like a bank. This new paradigm means reduced costs, faster transaction times, and increased accessibility for those without access to traditional financial institutions.

Take Bitcoin, for example. It operates on a peer-to-peer network that allows transactions to occur directly between users. The Bitcoin network itself is decentralized, meaning that no single user or organization controls it. Instead, numerous independently operated nodes in a network reach consensus, validating and recording transactions. This setup increases security since an attacker would need to control the majority of these nodes to compromise the network, a task so demanding and costly that it's practically unfeasible.

Tokens on a blockchain serve various functions, each integral to the ecosystem. They ensure network security, represent digital assets, and facilitate functions such as voting or governance in decentralized systems. For instance, in Ethereum—a platform that builds upon Bitcoin's foundation—smart contracts allow parties to set terms that execute automatically once certain conditions are met. This eliminates misunderstandings because of its programmatic nature and opens up possibilities for complex, conditional transactions. Ethereum is also the home of decentralized applications, or dApps, which offer services without centralized ownership, allowing for innovative solutions in fields from finance to social media.

Within these systems, 'miners' play an essential role. In networks like Bitcoin, miners validate transactions through a process known as proof of work. They solve complex mathematical problems, enabling verification without the need for a central authority. This is essential for maintaining the integrity and trustworthiness of the blockchain. On the other hand, Ethereum is transitioning to a proof-of-stake system where validators are chosen based on the number of tokens they hold and are willing to 'stake' or commit as a show of their investment in the network's success. This evolution showcases the adaptability and progressive change inherent in the crypto world.

But why decentralization? Beyond the technicalities, the ideology behind decentralization speaks to democratization and empowerment. It aims to disrupt traditional power structures within finance by offering financial services to the unbanked or underbanked. With a smartphone and internet connection, individuals across the globe can participate in an economy previously inaccessible to them, accessing everything from microloans to international money transfers without exorbitant fees.

A common concern and question often raised about cryptocurrencies is their inherent volatility and the lack of understanding about their operational mechanisms. The good news is that, slowly but surely, increased education and widespread adoption help mitigate these concerns. Institutional interest, for instance, brings a level of credibility to the sector that dissipates some skepticism. Furthermore, the rise of regulated exchanges and custodial services provides users with safer options to invest and trade.

Now, let's tackle some token utilities with real-life examples. Ethereum's ecosystem, with its smart contract capabilities, leads the pack. One renowned application is Uniswap, a decentralized exchange that lets anyone trade tokens without an order book. This democratization of exchange services allows for freedom and fluidity unseen in traditional finance, bypassing the need for costly brokerage fees or lengthy sign-ups.

Moreover, decentralized finance, or DeFi, transcends geographical boundaries, allowing users to borrow or lend cryptocurrencies without a middleman. Platforms like Compound and Aave let users earn interest by lending out their crypto, providing solutions in a space devoid of physical constraints. Additionally, tokens like Dai and USDC, known as stablecoins, aim to mitigate volatility by pegging to stable assets like the US dollar, offering a safer store of value for everyday transactions.

Understanding these concepts and applications requires pushing past the jargon and focusing on the practical implications of cryptocurrency and decentralization. For individuals entering the space, it's essential to understand the technical fundamentals to engage safely and knowledgeably. Cryptocurrencies offer a vision of financial inclusivity, adaptability, and unprecedented control over one's financial future.

We must acknowledge challenges, from regulatory concerns to technological scalability. However, these challenges drive innovation and problem-solving, leading to continuous improvements in the blockchain environment. As the technology matures, so do the debates about data privacy, security, and ethical implications. There's room for everyone to contribute to this conversation, helping shape a balanced space that considers both innovation and responsibility.

This section aims to breakdown complex concepts without oversimplification, focusing on a clear depiction of what decentralization within cryptocurrency means today and what it could mean in the future. As knowledge deepens and more individuals engage with the ecosystem, the potential for cryptocurrencies to integrate into the modern financial system grows. Through tokens, decentralized networks, and innovative solutions, the space not only challenges the status quo but also opens dialogue about the future of money.

Concluding Thoughts

Understanding the origins and foundational concepts of cryptocurrency equips us to better grasp its revolutionary role in reshaping modern financial systems. As we navigate through this digital transformation, it becomes evident that cryptocurrencies are not merely digital alternatives to money but powerful tools that challenge traditional financial structures. The combination of cryptography, decentralization, and blockchain offers a landscape where financial transactions are more secure, transparent, and accessible than ever before. This new terrain opens significant opportunities for innovation and inclusion, providing individuals and businesses with alternatives to conventional banking systems. Now that we recognize these core principles, we can appreciate how cryptocurrencies hold the potential to democratize finance and foster economic empowerment globally. By delving deeper into their implications and applications, we set the stage for harnessing their full potential, transforming how value is exchanged and creating pathways to a more inclusive financial future.

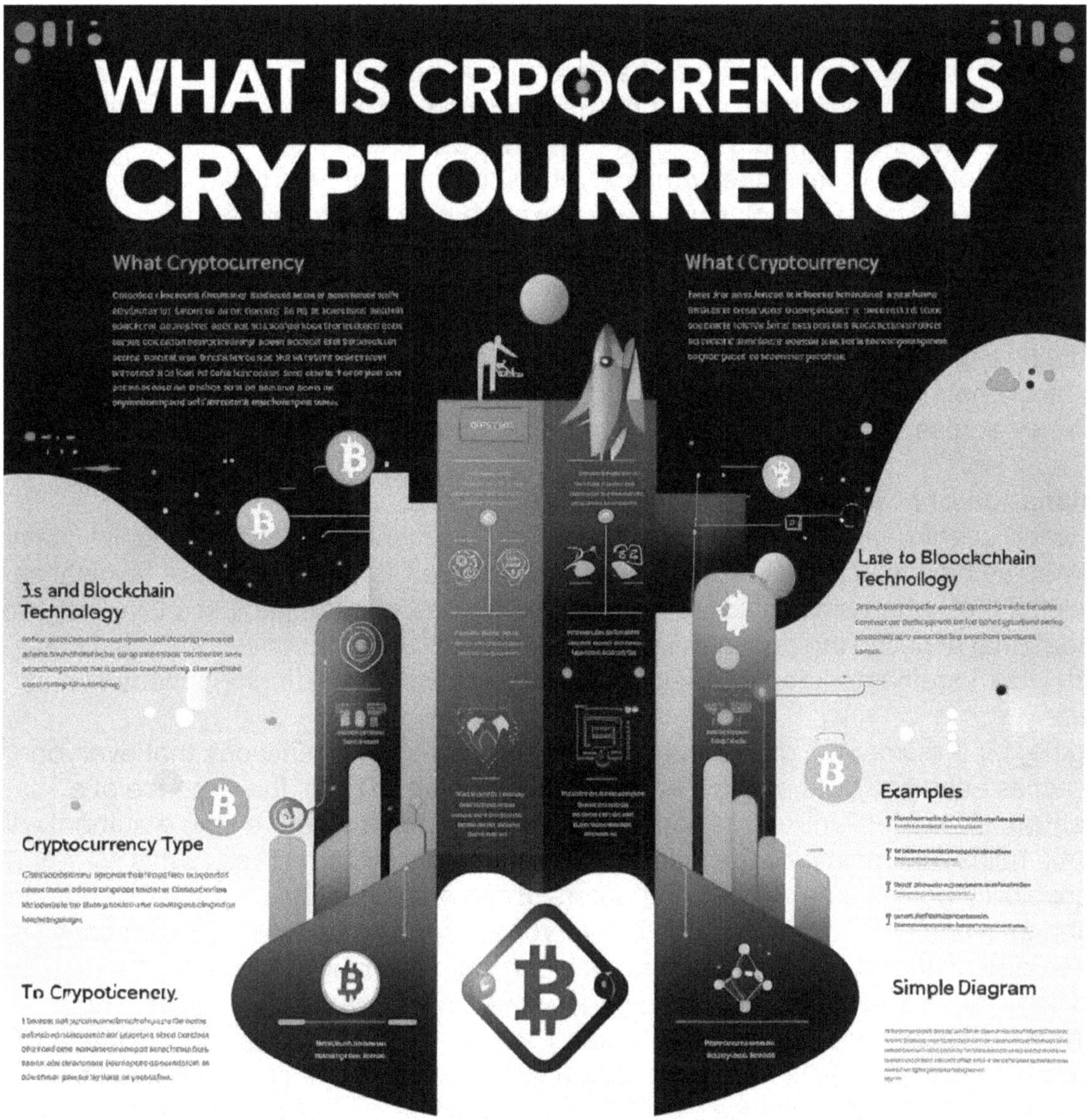

WHAT IS CRPØCRENCY IS
CRYPTOURRENCY
What Cryptocurrency
What (Cryptourrency
3.s and Blockchain Technology
Lɜıe to Blockchain Technology
Examples
Cryptocurrency Type
Simple Diagram
Tr Crypoticenely.

Chapter 2: *The Technology Behind the Revolution*

The Technology Behind the Revolution

"Imagine standing in a bustling marketplace, surrounded by people speaking different languages, busy exchanging goods and ideas. Amidst this chaos, every transaction relies heavily on trust—trust that the apples you're buying are fresh, trust that the money you're using is genuine, and trust that no one is trying to cheat you. However, what if there was a way to conduct all these transactions without relying on any trust at all? A system where everything is recorded transparently on a digital ledger in real-time, creating an environment where deception finds no place to hide.

In this chapter, we'll unravel the complex yet fascinating technology behind blockchain—the engine driving this revolution. We will explore how blockchain secures transactions through cryptography, ensures transparency by making information accessible to all participants, and creates trustless systems where transactions are validated not by middlemen but by consensus. Whether you're new to the world of cryptocurrency or seeking to deepen your understanding, this chapter aims to demystify how blockchain operates as a powerful tool for fostering security, transparency, and efficiency across various industries."

Explanation of how blockchain technology operates

In a world overflowing with buzzwords and hype, "blockchain" often tops the list, leaving many scratching their heads. Yet, beneath the surface lies a foundation of fascinating principles that, when articulated clearly, unveils a world of potential. Let's dive into two foundational aspects: the decentralized ledger system and consensus mechanisms, which work together to keep this whole blockchain ecosystem running smoothly and securely.

Imagine, for a moment, a digital ledger—a shared book of transactions that everyone with access can see but no single entity can manipulate. This is the essence of a decentralized ledger. Unlike traditional centralized systems where a single authority, like a bank, holds and maintains the ledger, a decentralized system spreads this responsibility across a network of computers. Each participant has a copy of the entire ledger, so when one person updates it, everyone else must update their own copy. This widespread distribution is the heartbeat of blockchain's reliability and security.

Traditional databases often find themselves vulnerable because they're like single doorways guarded by a centralized keeper. Hackers need only breach one point. With blockchain, even if a hacker compromises a single participant's copy, the system remains secure. Why? Because discrepancies would be effortlessly highlighted when cross-referenced against other participants' records. This collaborative system embodies democratized trust—a concept where trust arises from shared verification rather than depending on a single authority's word. So, why does this matter? Imagine buying property and ensuring your ownership isn't at the whim of a potential mishandled or corrupted solitary record keeper. The appeal here is obvious, especially in areas where distrust in centralized institutions runs high.

Now, you might wonder, with all these participants maintaining copies, how do they agree on which transactions are legitimate? Enter consensus mechanisms. They are akin to democratic voting, where agreement emerges not from a leader's decree but through collective affirmation. Different blockchains employ various consensus methods, each with unique tricks to maintain network integrity. The most well-known is Proof of Work (PoW), where miners—special network participants—solve complex mathematical puzzles. These puzzles are hard to crack but easy for others to verify once solved. The first to complete a puzzle gets to add the next block of transactions, essentially voting in favor of their reality as the true state of the ledger. It's secure because while one puzzle might cost immense effort, verifying it demands minimal work from others.

But of course, PoW isn't without fault—it's energy-intensive and not environmentally friendly. Here's where alternates like Proof of Stake (PoS) gain traction. Instead of battling computations, validators—another name for network participants—are chosen to create blocks based on the number of coins they own or "stake." Here, wealth equals influence, as those with more stake have more to lose by acting dishonestly. It rewards those with vested interest in maintaining the network, making it more efficient than PoW in terms of energy usage.

It's like organizing a community garden. In PoW, everyone digs tirelessly to plant one tree, while PoS asks how many trees each person already maintains, choosing the one with the most to plant more. Both aim to plant trees, yet with different energy tolls and incentives. Beyond PoW and PoS, there are also hybrid models and newer consensus methods continually emerging, aiming to better solve the puzzle of decentralization with improved efficiency and fairness.

What's critical for newcomers and curious minds is understanding blockchain's ecosystem isn't just about cryptocurrency trading; it's about establishing a new kind of system—one that champions transparency, security, and collaboration, emerging robust from the absence of centralized control.

As we delve further, think about how essential it is for us to feel secure within this vast digital landscape. As our section concludes, consider how vital advanced cryptographic methods become in enhancing security. By harnessing the power of cryptographic hashing and ensuring the immutability of data, we step into discussions that unravel how blockchain fortifies itself against unauthorized changes. Continually evolving, blockchain leverages technologies like cryptographic hashing to bolster its defenses, creating systems not just innovative, but also resilient. Understanding these enhancements will underline the population's need to trust in the technology supporting our transactions, one sealed block at a time. This groundwork sets the stage for exploring how these components work together, shaping a digital ledger that not only hosts secure transactions but optimistically promises a more secure digital future.

Detailed look at blockchain's security features

From our previous exploration of blockchain's foundational workings, we saw how its decentralized ledger system and consensus mechanisms are crucial for ensuring reliability and trust. Building on that, we now delve into how these foundational elements of blockchain are further reinforced by cryptographic hashing and immutability to create a fortified security structure. At the heart of blockchain security is cryptographic hashing, which ensures that data integrity is steadfastly maintained. Each block on the blockchain contains a unique hash generated by a mathematical algorithm, efficiently creating a digital fingerprint of the data.

Imagine you secure a box of documents by locking it with a unique key created from the contents of the box itself. Cryptographic hashing functions in a similar way. When you input any piece of data, a cryptographic hash function generates a fixed-size alphanumeric hash value. An example of this is the SHA-256 algorithm, widely used in many blockchain systems. The beauty and power of hashing are illustrated by its one-way functionality—meaning that it's easy to convert data into a hash, but nearly impossible to reverse the process. Change just a single character in your data, and the resulting hash is completely different; this property is known as "avalanche effect." Due to this characteristic, if anyone tries to tamper with the original data, the mismatch with the associated hash becomes instantly apparent.

Immutability is a natural companion to cryptographic hashing. Picture entering data into a physical ledger, where every entry must be signed and approved before the page is laminated; that's akin to blockchain's immutability. Once a transaction is verified and added to the blockchain, it becomes etched in digital stone. Altering a past entry recasts all subsequent entries, which would require recalibrating the cryptographic hash of each block—a feat virtually impossible with distributed consensus. If someone attempted to change the data in one block, the hash would change, throwing the entire chain's integrity into disarray. This assures participants that any transaction recorded on the blockchain is permanent and authentic.
The technology ensures that once the information is in, it’s in for good. Think of it like a diary written with permanent ink; attempts to edit what's been recorded would be obvious and noticeably disruptive. This unalterable aspect instills confidence among participants that once data is accepted, it cannot be maliciously modified without widespread consensus, making fraudulent activities virtually futile.

These cryptographic technologies uphold two pillars: data integrity and security within blockchain systems. They serve as watchful guardians, barring entry points to unscrupulous modifications. Cryptographic hashing continuously verifies data integrity, while immutability ensures that the data remains consistent over time. Together, they work in symbiosis, providing a security architecture that excellently safeguards against unauthorized access and fraudulent undertakings. The mere fact that an attempt to change the hashed data changes the entire block makes any deceitful efforts glaring.
To illustrate this dynamic duo at work, consider a scenario involving financial transactions on a blockchain network. Suppose a dishonest actor attempts to alter a transaction to reflect a different amount. Their first challenge would be to modify the transaction data, thereby invalidating the hash. Then, they must manage to recalculate the hashes for each subsequent block in the chain faster than the network can produce new blocks. In a decentralized system spread over numerous nodes, this task verges on impossible without colluding with the majority of these nodes, adding significant deterrence to fraud attempts. Ultimately, the immutable ledger ensures financial transactions remain incorruptible, underlining the formidable security offered by the blockchain.

Each element of blockchain technology functions like pieces of a grand security puzzle. If you consider each block as a brick strengthened with hashing and immutability, then the entire blockchain is akin to a fortified fortress. Attempting to breach this digital fortress is not only resource-intensive but also temporally unfeasible, due to the congruent cryptographic safeguarding. Every successful entry into the blockchain

further solidifies its unyielding nature.
In the conversation beyond, about the transparency aspect of blockchain technology, we'll see how every transaction led across this network is visible to all authorized participants. This transparency complements the strong security principles we've established. By ensuring all participants can independently verify the accuracy of each transaction, this openness equally deters foul play as much as immutability and hashing do. We'll further envision how transparency and security mutually reinforce one another to maintain integrity across blockchain systems, building a comprehensive picture of how blockchain technology reshapes trust and reliability in the digital space.
This dialogue reaffirms that each part of blockchain technology plays an essential role, contributing to a reliable, decentralized system where trust isn't a prerequisite but an inevitable outcome. As we progress to discuss transparency, we anticipate seeing how openly visible transactions foster a collaborative environment where trust is tangibly rooted in technology's robust structure.

Explore the transparency offered by blockchain technology
You have now discovered the world of cryptographic hashing and immutability, which collectively build a rock-solid foundation for security in blockchain technology. But security is like the first layer in the cake of transparency—what makes blockchain truly stand apart. Imagine having every action visible and accountable, like putting on glasses that allow you to see every key movement within an organization. That's transparency for you, woven into the fabric of blockchain. The public ledger sitting at the heart of blockchain generously unfolds its entries to anyone who participates, like reading a story where nothing is tucked away in secrecy.
Let's demystify how this works. Picture a giant, digital chalkboard accessible to everyone. Each transaction on a blockchain is written boldly and indelibly across this board. There's nothing opaque about it—every participant gets an equally clear view, making verification possible without needing a trusted bookstore ghostwriting assurances. Each record creates a chain of trust that anyone can audit, drastically minimizing the chances of nefarious activity lurking unnoticed.

Consider a common scenario: supply chains. Traditionally, the journey from raw material to retail product involves multiple opaque stages, each susceptible to errors or alteration. With blockchain, each stage—say, a shipment moving from a factory to the shelves—is logged as a transaction. These logs capture data like timestamps, locations, and authenticity details, knitting together an unbroken account visible to all stakeholders. No more misplaced goods magically vanishing or reappearing where they shouldn't. Transparency paints them into the ledger, leaving no wiggle room for manipulation. Every step is unequivocal, visible, and trustworthy.
Blockchain doesn't need complex technical terms to be effective—it leverages straightforward logic. Think of the blockchain as a diary that writes itself each time a new page (or block) is filled. Every writer (or node) has access to its history and verifies that the stories it holds are true, thanks to cryptographic proofs. It builds a system based on plain attributes: visibility, accessibility, and accountability, like a community library open to anyone wishing to read through its contents.
Does this transparency spawn questions about privacy? Absolutely, but it balances its openness with protocols that maintain user anonymity, ensuring private details remain undisclosed while validating transactions openly. You can still see what's happening

without peering into personal aspects—like viewing a vibrant picture while respecting the privacy of each brushstroke.
Blockchain's all-access pass to visibility ensures that the system operates without relying on the trust of strangers. By offering a clear window into transactional histories, it diffuses distrust, making users feel secure in knowing that no wizard is secretly pulling levers behind a curtain. Imagine a world where nobody doubts the conditions or existence of a signed agreement because everyone has a copy, verified endlessly and updated in real time by each participant—an everlasting digital handshake of trust.
Let's connect this with how blockchain champions prevent duplication and fraud: every transaction's visibility thwarts double-spending, essentially doing the same work twice and pretending it was just once. It makes running schemes extraordinarily difficult because any discrepancy lights up like a warning beacon, there for each node to spot and challenge.

Not stopping at financial transactions, blockchain's transparency translates magnificently into areas like healthcare. Patient information, once recorded, can be shared securely among doctors and specialists, easily updateable and traceable back through time. A seamless interaction emerges, showing the real-time status of health data without disrupting privacy norms or inducing layers of bureaucracy.
As transparency takes center stage, it sets the scene for another incredible phenomenon: trustless systems. The open-book nature of blockchain naturally leads us here. Seen and verified by all, transactions glide without intermediaries. The open ledger forms the spine for trustless environments, where every accord is machine-verified, cutting down the need for trusting that someone's word is their bond.
By letting visibility flourish within its operation, blockchain doesn't just chart transactions—it crafts integrity. Every line of the public ledger is a glowing testament to accountability, a clear mirror reflecting the interminable process of honesty. It proposes a transformative shift that traditional ledgers couldn't achieve, using transparency as a lynchpin.
Picture a giant tapestry of interwoven interactions, each peer reviewing the other, omniscient and impartial. Blockchain gives individuals and companies alike an unprecedented degree of confidence that what they see reported is indeed the complete unvarnished truth.

It's time to look beyond and glimpse the genesis of trustless systems—a concept incubated by transparency. Armed with open ledgers, these systems slough off the need for middlemen. It's where blockchain promises the future of direct, reliable engagement. While across the sky of transactional worlds different models may yet play their part, in the theater of blockchain commerce, every stakeholder plays a key role in enforcing the authenticity we all seek.
In essence, transparency is more than just seeing through; it's about revealing, comprehending, and approving. It's about accepting this gift that ensures the skepticism of the unknown can be quashed by the certainty of the known. This component doesn't merely support the architecture of blockchain: it galvanizes it. Through these visible transactions, we move towards a seamless existence of trustless exchanges, where certainty doesn't knock, it lounges in certainty's home. Prepared to venture into trustless realms, understanding transparency gives you the keys.
Understanding trustless systems within blockchain

Let's begin by revisiting our discussion on transparency in blockchain systems. Transparency allows every transaction to be visible to everyone in the network, which is absolutely essential as a foundation for trustless interactions. This transparency ensures that each participant can verify transactions without relying on a central authority. If you think about it, transparency means everything is out in the open, giving each party confidence that transactions occur precisely as they appear. This is crucial in fostering environments where trust is based on what you can verify rather than what someone tells you to trust.

Now, let's dive into the heart of this section: trustless interactions enabled by blockchain technology. Blockchain fundamentally changes the way transactions are conducted by removing intermediaries, leading to a shift in where we place our trust—from central entities to the network itself. In traditional systems, we require intermediaries such as banks or brokers to ensure that transactions are legitimate. These middlemen serve as the guarantors of trust, ensuring both parties fulfill their obligations. However, they also bring about inefficiencies, costs, and potential risks associated with centralized control. In blockchain, trustless does not mean the absence of trust; rather, it indicates that trust is established differently. The technology uses decentralized consensus mechanisms, like proof of work or proof of stake, to verify transactions. This verification is done by the network as a whole, rather than a single central authority. These mechanisms ensure that all nodes in the network agree on the validity of each transaction before it is added to the blockchain. Once confirmed, transactions are virtually immutable and transparent, further reinforcing trust within the system. For instance, Bitcoin transactions are validated by mining, where miners solve complex mathematical puzzles to add blocks to the blockchain. These puzzles require significant computational effort, and their difficulty ensures that the majority of miners must agree on a transaction's validity before it is approved.

The implications of this shift are immense. Without the need for intermediaries, transactions can occur more rapidly and with reduced costs. Think of how blockchain can disrupt industries such as finance, real estate, or supply chain management, where middlemen currently play a crucial role. For example, in finance, smart contracts—self-executing contracts with terms directly written into code—execute transactions automatically upon meeting predefined conditions. This automation reduces the need for lawyers or banks to mediate, enhancing efficiency and reliability.

Trustless interactions also have a significant security dimension. By decentralizing the transaction validation process, blockchain technology mitigates risks associated with single-point failures characteristic of centralized systems. If one node in a blockchain network is compromised, the consensus mechanism ensures that the network's overall integrity isn't affected because other nodes uphold the validation process. This distribution of trust across multiple nodes makes blockchain networks resilient to attacks, a vital feature for industries handling sensitive data.

Moreover, when we talk about the international transfer of funds, traditional banking systems can be slow and expensive, often taking several days to clear due to the involvement of numerous intermediaries. Blockchain provides a faster, cost-effective alternative, facilitating nearly instantaneous transactions without banks. Consider remittances, where the cost and time of transferring money from one country to another have historically been significant. Blockchain simplifies this process, reducing both fees and transfer times, which is particularly beneficial for individuals in developing countries relying on remittances for their livelihood.

We should also consider how blockchain's trustless nature can invite new avenues for innovation. By decentralizing trust, small businesses and entrepreneurs have more opportunities to participate in global markets without facing barriers like high transaction fees or access to trusted intermediaries. This equalizing effect can drive innovation and create more competitive markets.

While trustless interactions offer numerous benefits, they also bring challenges and considerations. The technology's novelty and complexity pose barriers to adoption, especially for those lacking technical expertise. Educating stakeholders about blockchain and developing a regulatory framework remain essential in building a comprehensive trustless ecosystem.

As this section on trustless interactions winds down, it’s crucial to see how everything ties into what comes next. We'll explore how security, transparency, and trustless systems work hand-in-hand to build a cohesive blockchain environment. Security ensures that the data on the blockchain remains intact, transparency ensures that each transaction is visible to all, and trustless interactions allow for secure transactions without intermediaries. Together, they create robust, reliable structures where innovation can thrive without compromising safety or transparency. Understanding these components' interplay is important to grasp blockchain's broader implications for industries and societies.

In summary, trustless interactions in blockchain illustrate a profound shift in trust paradigms, empowering individuals over centralized entities and ensuring transactions' integrity through a decentralized, transparent network. By rendering intermediaries obsolete, blockchain fosters efficiency, reduces costs, and invites innovation. Nevertheless, realizing its full potential depends on advancing understanding, addressing regulatory challenges, and promoting wider adoption. As we move forward, how these elements integrate will shape blockchain's future, underscoring the crucial conversation on its transformative impact.

The interplay between security, transparency, and trustless systems in blockchain

Building on trustless interactions, we see that blockchain architecture is fundamentally designed to function without the need for trust between participants. Security enhances this by ensuring that all transactions are secure from alteration or interference. At its core, blockchain employs cryptographic methods to lock transactions, making individual transactions and overall data history immutable. This security framework not only guards against tampering but also prevents unauthorized access, which is a common vulnerability in traditional systems.

Transparency complements this trustless and secure structure by providing an open window into the blockchain's entire operation. Unlike conventional transaction methods that require a trusted third party, blockchain achieves transparency by having all transactions recorded on a distributed ledger. Every participant on the network has access to this ledger. They actively verify the transactions, ensuring they are conducted according to agreed-upon protocols. This visibility provides users with confidence because they can track and trace the path of their transactions without relying on a third party's word.

Consider the example of financial transactions, a sector where security, transparency, and trustless operations are critical. In traditional banking, people must rely on banks as trusted intermediaries to confirm transaction validity. Blockchain eliminates this need. Security mechanisms such as hashing and digital signatures ensure that once a transaction is made, it is indelibly etched into the blockchain's history. Similarly, transparency allows every participant to witness each transaction's flow, providing a trustless and peer-verified method of operation.

The role of blockchain in preventing fraud illustrates how these elements come together. Fraud typically occurs in systems where users lack the ability to verify authenticity independently. Let's take supply chain management as a specific example. Blockchain records each step of the product journey, from manufacturing to delivery, creating an auditable and transparent chain. Each participant adds a block of information, verified by consensus within the network. By making this process visible to all parties, blockchain eliminates the opaqueness that leads to fraud.

As we delve deeper into blockchain's applications, its potential to transform governance becomes evident. Traditional government systems rely heavily on intermediaries to manage records, whether they're related to voting or public resources. This reliance can lead to inefficiencies and lack of transparency. Blockchain systems, however, provide a secure and tamper-proof base that records the details of every interaction, decision, or transaction. When citizens can independently verify that their vote is counted, faith in electoral processes increases, encouraging more democratic participation.

Apart from finance and governance, the applications of blockchain technology are rapidly expanding into other fields. In healthcare, for instance, patient records demand high levels of security and confidentiality. Here, blockchain safeguards sensitive health data against breaches by encrypting records, allowing only authorized access through cryptographic keys. The transparency of blockchain further assures patients that their records have not been altered, as any changes would need to be validated by the network.

Similarly, in real estate, blockchain systems can streamline property transactions. Traditionally, a property purchase involves multiple parties—buyers, sellers, agents, lenders—all trusting external registries to verify ownership and transaction legitimacy. Blockchain consolidates ownership data into a single ledger that is both viewable and verifiable by all parties involved. The inherent security and transparency eliminate the need for title insurance and lengthy bureaucratic processes, leading to faster and more secure transactions.

As we examine these examples, the interplay between trustless systems, security, and transparency becomes clear. Each element on its own could improve systems, but together they transform how entities operate. The collaborative nature of blockchain not only mitigates fraud but also reassures all stakeholders that their interests are protected. Therefore, industries can design more efficient, reliable processes, regardless of the sector.

The expansion of smart contracts within blockchain provides another layer that improves efficiency and strength of trustless systems. These contracts automatically execute transactions when predefined conditions are met. They eliminate the need for a gatekeeper, securing the transaction without any intermediary. This mechanism exemplifies the blockchain's security, since once the contract is coded, it cannot be altered without consensus. Transparency is inherent as every contract action is

recorded on the blockchain, visible to all parties involved.
Despite these advances, widespread adoption of blockchain technology does face challenges such as scalability, energy consumption, and regulatory compliance. Ensuring blockchain can handle a volume of transactions comparable to traditional systems remains a focus. Technologies like sharding and the transition from proof of work to proof of stake show promise in addressing these challenges, making blockchain more scalable and less energy-intensive. As governments continue to explore these technologies, regulations will evolve to support these innovations, ensuring compliance with security and confidentiality standards.

In conclusion, by combining trustless environments with unyielding security and transparency, blockchain offers a robust framework for modern digital transactions. The synergies between these elements create systems resistant to fraud, capable of inspiring confidence among users. As blockchain continues to evolve, its foundational principles will underpin innovations across a multitude of domains, heralding an era where trusted intermediaries become a relic of the past. In this ecosystem, users themselves become the pivotal assurance of reliability and integrity in a decentralized, open digital age.

Bringing It All Together

As we now grasp the intricate yet fascinating mechanics of blockchain technology, the road ahead is paved with possibilities that promise a secure, transparent, and inherently trustless digital landscape. Understanding these core principles equips us to imagine our future interactions—from financial systems that reduce reliance on middlemen to groundbreaking innovations in industries like healthcare, real estate, and governance. For crypto newcomers, professionals, educators, and policymakers alike, this knowledge serves as a catalyst to explore how blockchain can redefine security and transparency across all sectors. Equipped with this insight, we have the foundation to venture confidently into a digital world where transactions are not only safe but also accessible to all, fostering an environment ripe for growth and innovation.

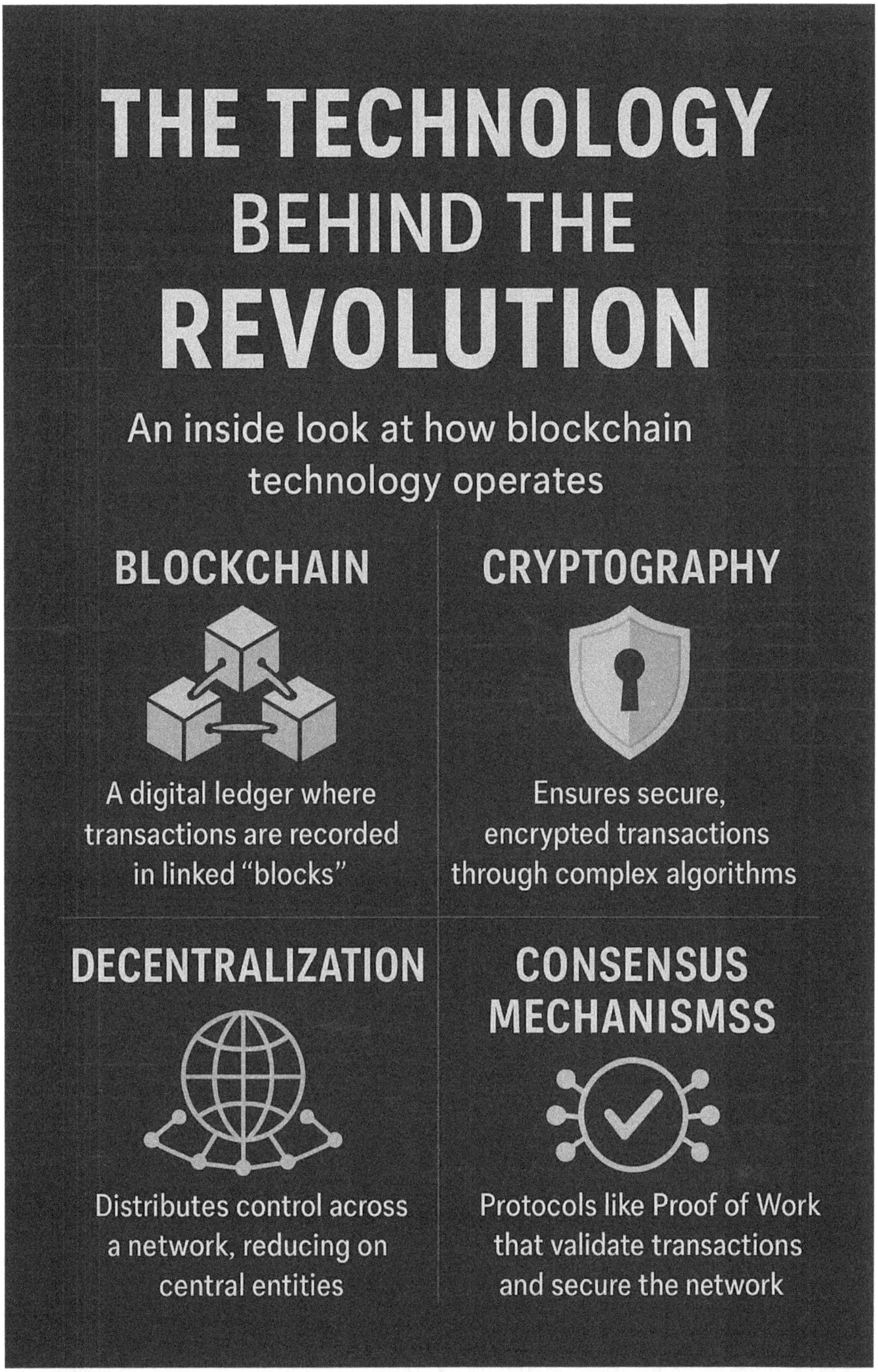
THE TECHNOLOGY BEHIND THE REVOLUTION
An inside look at how blockchain technology operates
BLOCKCHAIN
A digital ledger where transactions are recorded in linked "blocks"
CRYPTOGRAPHY
Ensures secure, encrypted transactions through complex algorithms
DECENTRALIZATION
Distributes control across a network, reducing on central entities
CONSENSUS MECHANISMSS
Protocols like Proof of Work that validate transactions and secure the network

Chapter 3: *Crypto vs. Traditional Finance*

Crypto vs. Traditional Finance

Imagine you're standing in line at a bank, waiting your turn to deposit a small amount of money. The line inches forward slowly as you glance at the clock on the wall, feeling the weight of time slip away. This is not an unfamiliar scene for many around the world who rely on traditional financial systems. The process often involves paperwork and fees that make even simple transactions a cumbersome ordeal. Meanwhile, a friend in another part of town taps their smartphone, sending payment in seconds without stepping foot outside. This contrast between the old and the new highlights the evolving landscape of finance today.

In a rapidly changing world where speed, accessibility, and cost are crucial, both traditional and crypto systems offer unique advantages and challenges. This chapter will explore these contrasting systems by examining how they impact global access to financial services, addressing the needs of unbanked and underbanked populations. With a focus on operational aspects, we'll navigate how these financial landscapes aim to empower users differently, inviting a closer look into the narratives shaping modern finance.

Introduction to Crypto vs. Traditional Finance

Cryptocurrency and traditional finance cater to our perpetual quest for ways to save, transfer, and grow money, each carrying its own narrative. Traditional finance is like an ancient city, built with the laws of equilibrium, operating for centuries, its roots stretching deep into history. Banks, central banks, and regulatory bodies are the architects of this city, cultivating security and trust through oversight and rule of law. Most of us are accustomed to it, managing our finances through banks for loans or investments, trusting their solidity. Imagine a vast network, where reliability prevails, but often comes with bureaucracy and often rigid procedures. Established fiat currencies like dollars and euros dominate this realm, issuing paper money and maintaining value through governmental authority.

On the other side, cryptocurrency emerges as the new kid on the block, decentralized, and defined best by unpredictability and innovation. It was born from the ideology of breaking free from centralized control, aiming to democratize finance through transparency. Bitcoin, the poster child of crypto, introduced this idea around 2009. These digital currencies live on the blockchain, a secure and public ledger, eliminating intermediaries and supposedly empowering users with greater currency control. Ethereum, another major player, expanded cryptos beyond just financial transactions into a platform for decentralized applications. This represents a mosaic of coding and cryptography resulting in privacy, efficiency, and global outreach, yet often perplexing for those unfamiliar.

Diverging from one another, both systems present unique frameworks. Philosophy divides them first; traditional finance relies on centralized trust and stability, invoking long-standing traditions. Cryptocurrency challenges this by advocating decentralization, where trust springs from complex algorithms. Structurally, in traditional finance, banks hold central databases for records, balancing between security and accessibility.

Cryptocurrencies use distributed ledgers, meaning that countless copies of their transaction records exist simultaneously worldwide, theoretically bolstering security yet also introducing volatility.
Operationally, traditional finance is bound by opening hours, days laced with paperwork and bureaucracy, and geographical constraints. This contrasts with cryptocurrency's 24/7 nature, embodying speed where transactions occur within minutes, breaking limitations of borders. However, this speed invites risk, with security concerns where losing a digital key might mean losing access to one's assets permanently.
You might envision a merchant in a bustling city square for clarity. They face a traditional choice, where transactions need bank mediation to process credit card payments, often at a fee. Conversely, visualize them accepting Bitcoin, bypassing banks, and interactions morph into swift exchanges with lower costs. Cryptocurrency, thus, extends its hand as a reduction in transactional friction, but trust issues emerge; values fluctuate unpredictably with few safeguards against loss.

Another disparity in their philosophy lies in the regulatory landscape. Traditional finance is stringently overseen, their actions scrutinized by governmental policy and international laws, constructing a safety net for users. Cryptocurrencies, although facing their growing scrutiny, primarily remain a landslide of less regulation, appealing to those seeking escape from government prying but also subjecting themselves to a wild west environment where potential for misuse looms.
Despite their disparities, both systems entice us to reflect on our financial inclinations, engaging diverse audiences, from curious minds venturing into digital territories to seasoned professionals weighing new paths. Younger generations, tech-savvy and unperturbed by digital transformations, find cryptos intriguing. Investors double down, chasing the next big rise, desiring alternative avenues away from traditional stock markets and commodity trading.
Professionals and entrepreneurs stretch towards digital currencies, employing the speed for cross-border transactions without traditional hoops. They see potential in cryptos' promise to level the economic playing field while weighing associated risks. Students look to this arena as a treasure trove of knowledge, preparing to innovate within or beyond the financial spectrum. Policy makers and development practitioners observe closely, as crypto holds promise and peril, challenging systemic norms and calling for potential integration and regulation.

Real-world applications of these systems lay bare their capabilities and limitations. Traditional finance keeps our homes warm and loans accessible in the norm most seek. Cryptocurrencies possess a different allure—glimpsing into social causes, sending Bitcoin to aid groups bypasses red tape, revolutionizing donations in crisis scenarios. Looking towards what's next, this chapter intends to bring forth the overarching theme of financial inclusion, portraying how both systems, despite differences, strive for accessibility across global demarcations. With traditional banking systems attempting to penetrate remote regions and cryptocurrencies blazing trails even in infrastructure-starved areas, digital inclusivity becomes a shared dictum.
A swift pivot allows us to delve into these next steps, alluding to this expanding accessibility. Traditional finance fortifies infrastructures, while cryptocurrency seeks to topple predicaments through digital means. We'll tread this path to better grasp how each financial system stands as a beacon amidst the evolving dialogue of today's

financial landscape.

Accessibility in Crypto vs. Traditional Finance

The previous section laid the groundwork by comparing the structural contrasts between cryptocurrencies and traditional finance systems. These two distinct frameworks differ in their foundational approaches to managing and facilitating financial transactions. Now, we delve into their accessibility on a global scale, shedding light on how these systems cater to diverse populations and regions.

Cryptocurrencies represent a new frontier in global financial accessibility. Unlike traditional banks, which rely on physical infrastructure and regulatory frameworks, cryptocurrencies leap over geographical boundaries through digital platforms accessible by anyone with an internet connection. This capability is transformative, potentially closing gaps that conventional banks struggle to bridge. Traditional banks require physical branches, extensive paperwork, and often exclude individuals who lack formal identification or credit history. In contrast, cryptocurrencies eliminate many of these barriers. Platforms like Bitcoin and Ethereum offer access simply through wallets that one can set up online with minimal information.

The geographical reach of cryptocurrencies outweighs that of traditional banking in many underserved regions. Consider rural areas in developing countries where the nearest bank branch might be hours away. Here, digital currencies provide a practical alternative, turning a simple smartphone into a financial toolkit. For instance, in parts of Africa, cryptocurrencies have gained traction as a method to store and transfer value, effectively bypassing the need for a local financial institution. This scenario highlights direct access to financial services, enabling even the most isolated individuals to participate in the global economy.

Cryptocurrencies offer hope for the unbanked and underbanked populations. Without access to traditional account services, these groups face hurdles to economic participation. Digital currencies present solutions tailored to their needs. With little required to set up an account, they enable individuals to save money, receive payments, and perform transactions without a traditional bank's infrastructure. Initiatives like Stellar and initiatives built on blockchain technology ensure that people can transfer money quickly and affordably. These services are particularly beneficial in regions where remittances from family members abroad form a large part of household income. One vivid example is the Philippines, where a sizable portion of the population works overseas, sending money home. Traditional remittances are costly and slow due to transaction fees and the time needed for money to clear. However, by using cryptocurrencies, this process is streamlined. Blockchain's efficiency allows for real-time, low-cost transfers, giving families immediate access to funds and reducing financial stress.

Digital inclusivity further extends through initiatives developed within the cryptocurrency space aimed at empowering the underbanked. For example, projects like Celo focus on providing financial tools accessible from basic mobile devices. Celo's mobile-first strategy lowers barriers for people less technologically adept or without laptops. Their efforts illustrate how crypto platforms adapt to users' environments instead of expecting users to adapt to them. These projects do more than serve as banks; they enhance financial literacy, allowing individuals to better manage their financial future.

In emerging economies, where the internet has outpaced banking infrastructure, cryptocurrencies reach out to those left behind. Some nations have embraced Bitcoin as legal tender, promoting a decentralized system that coexists with traditional monetary frameworks. This step endorses a mixed-model approach that further boosts financial inclusion. Such actions affirm the potential of cryptocurrencies to deliver on promises of comprehensive access.

Engagement with crypto also educates on managing value beyond just holding and transferring it. For instance, decentralized finance (DeFi) platforms present a way for users to earn returns on their holdings, transitioning from basic inclusion to participation in more complex financial activities. This shift increases economic empowerment by leveraging crypto's capability to extend services like lending, borrowing, and investing to those traditionally excluded.

Though traditional banks argue the advantages of regulatory safeguards and consumer protection, which cryptocurrencies are still navigating, the flexibility and reach of digital currencies challenge these systems to rethink their inclusivity. In fact, some banks have started partnerships with fintech firms to integrate digital currencies. This collaboration bridges traditional finance's credibility with cryptocurrency's reach, taking strategic approaches to expand their customer bases in innovative ways.

As this analysis of accessibility concludes, it opens up the door to considering transaction speeds. In the chapters ahead, the discussion will focus on comparing the efficiencies and speed that cryptocurrencies can offer. In many situations, these digital assets promise real-time processing benefits, contrasting the often slow and sometimes cumbersome processes of traditional banking. By addressing these aspects, the narrative continues to explore the stark differences and emerging synergies between these two financial domains.

Speed of Transactions in Crypto vs. Traditional Finance

In the previous section, we explored how global access to financial services opens doors to empowerment for those historically underserved by traditional banking systems. This access is pivotal to the broader question of how efficiently these systems operate. Stepping into this section, we find transaction speed sitting at the heart of this investigation. Both crypto and traditional finance promise inclusivity, yet the speed at which transactions conclude significantly influences their practicality and user satisfaction.

Cryptocurrencies, with their near-instantaneous transaction capabilities, offer a sharp contrast to the more cumbersome processes of traditional banks. Bitcoin transactions, for instance, can be completed in a matter of minutes, even seconds in some cases, whereas an international bank transfer might linger for several days. This speed isn't just a matter of convenience—it can be transformative. Picture a business needing to pay an overseas supplier swiftly to release goods for delivery. With cryptocurrencies, this transaction can happen in real time, potentially reducing delays in the supply chain and avoiding costly downtime.

The impact on global remittances is even more profound. Many rely heavily on sending money across borders to support families or settle financial commitments. Traditional methods often involve complex networks and intermediaries, each adding time and cost. Crypto transactions, by contrast, can leap over these hurdles, landing in the recipient's digital wallet almost as swiftly as sending an email. For those without access to a local bank, such speed can mean the difference between purchasing essential

supplies on time or facing unwanted shortages.
Speed affects not just efficiency but user experience and financial planning as well. The ability to manage funds in real-time allows for more accurate forecasting and budgeting, something individuals and businesses alike can appreciate. Imagine you're a small business owner tracking cash flow. Real-time visibility of funds in transit gives you an advantage, allowing for nimble decision-making. The same holds true for personal finance; knowing your money has transferred without delay helps manage daily expenses and commitments with ease.
Technological advancements in crypto are largely behind this acceleration. The decentralized nature of blockchain means transactions bypass the elaborate multi-step processes involving banks and clearing houses. Yet, it's not without challenges. Network congestion can slow down crypto transactions. Additionally, high transaction volumes can lead to increased fees, which is something developers are constantly striving to mitigate. Despite these limitations, the trajectory of improvement continues to tilt favorably toward more stable and efficient operations.

A faster transaction cycle also fosters broader financial inclusion. For those devoid of access to traditional banking, the immediacy offered by crypto is a strong allure. In regions where banking infrastructure is sparse or unreliable, the potential to engage economically without delay empowers individuals and businesses alike. This real-time capability represents more than speed—it's about eliminating barriers to entry and participating on equal footing with someone miles away. A farmer in Ghana can transact with a supplier in China without a hitch or a high cost, opening opportunities previously reserved for only a privileged few.
Turning to traditional banking, the good old methods that have stood for decades continue to face scrutiny for their pace. While strides have been made to quicken transfers, especially domestically, crossing borders remains painfully slow. Many wonder if these systems lack the agility to compete in today's fast-paced economy. The question arises: are they doing enough to innovate, or will they be left in the dust by nimbler, tech-driven solutions? Traditional financial institutions are increasingly aware of the need to move faster, but the structural transformation required is ongoing and complex.
Cryptocurrencies, on the other hand, provide a glimpse of what's possible when legacy systems don't bound innovation. The instant nature of transactions buttressed by blockchain technology cuts through red tape, offering a leaner mechanism for moving value. There's an excitement here akin to the early days of the internet—a new frontier promising endless possibilities where speed is as much about accessibility as it is about the democratization of finance.

As we transition to the next section, we'll shift our focus to the cost implications and service fees inherent in both crypto and traditional systems. Speed is crucial, but its role must be balanced with the financial implications users face in each system.
Understanding these costs lays a foundation for assessing the user preference and decision-making landscape. While speedy transactions light the way, the real value choice arises when speed and cost intersect. As you'll soon discover, what you pay is as vital as how quickly you transact.

Cost Comparisons between Crypto and Traditional Finance

Examining the intricacies of transaction speed leads us directly to the financial implications of using cryptocurrencies compared to traditional financial systems. At the heart of the crypto revolution lies a promise of reduced transaction costs that challenge the status quo of everyday banking. One immediate and compelling contrast is between traditional bank transfer fees and cryptocurrency transaction fees. Banks typically charge for domestic transfers, and these charges increase when dealing with international transfers, often containing hidden fees and unfavorable exchange rates. In comparison, cryptocurrencies offer a direct, peer-to-peer nature that usually attracts lower fees, often irrespective of geographical boundaries. This means for those frequently sending money abroad, the difference in fees could translate to significant savings.

To illustrate, let's consider a standard wire transfer. Sending money internationally through traditional banks can incur fees up to $50 or more, depending on the bank and the countries involved. In contrast, sending the equivalent amount via a cryptocurrency like Bitcoin might only cost a few dollars, depending on the network's congestion. Moreover, these fees tend to scale with transaction size in banks, while in crypto, they often remain fixed or vary less drastically, opening the door for businesses and individuals to save considerably when moving substantial amounts of money routinely.

Service fees present another area ripe for cost-cutting through crypto. Conventional finance institutions impose a variety of service fees, from account maintenance charges to penalties for not meeting minimum balance requirements or exceeding withdrawal limits. They also charge heftily for services like foreign currency exchanges or overseas card payments, which can be financially draining. Crypto platforms, however, often skip these routine charges. They don't require account maintenance fees, and using a crypto wallet is usually free. When it comes to foreign transactions, cryptocurrencies bypass the need for complex foreign exchange procedures, typically incurring minimal conversion costs if any at all.

Consider a scenario where a person travels frequently for work. Using traditional banking services, they'd face currency conversion fees and ATM withdrawal costs abroad, quickly adding up over multiple trips. With crypto, they can hold a universal digital currency that doesn't compel them to navigate frequent conversions each time they favor spending a local currency. This latitude can substantially enhance savings and financial planning, streamlining expenses that, cumulatively, can represent a considerable portion of a savvy traveler's budget.

The broader financial benefits for users who invest in cryptocurrencies over traditional currencies amplify these savings. In the long run, users often find they can save a considerable amount on routine transactions alone. Furthermore, the decentralized nature of crypto also shields users from some risks tied to conventional banking systems, such as account freezes and transaction restrictions. These flexibilities contribute to peace of mind, which is not always quantifiable in pure financial terms but adds a palpable layer of value to one's financial experience.

We see scenarios across tech-savvy communities where young professionals turn to crypto for favorable returns and practical benefits. One vivid example involves gig economy workers, particularly those in regions with volatile economies. Traditional banking often binds these individuals with restrictions, hidden costs, and bureaucratic hitches. Cryptocurrency allows these workers to maneuver financial waters freely, sidestepping such constraints and enjoying newfound autonomy with their finances. A freelancer receiving payments in crypto can sidestep volatile fiat fluctuations, converting only portions needed for immediate expenses while potentially benefiting from price appreciation.

One might wonder how reliable these cost benefits are. Well, while cryptocurrencies can come with network fees, especially in times of high network use, the development of scaling solutions like the Lightning Network seeks to mitigate these spikes by enabling rapid transactions at a fraction of the cost. This consistent push for improvement in the crypto infrastructure signifies a genuine commitment to ensuring cost-effectiveness remains a centerpiece of the financial experience.

The crypto economy subsequently carves out a more financially inclusive space, particularly for those who remain underserved by traditional systems. Consider someone without access to formal identification or credit history; traditional banks might find them unsuitable. Cryptocurrency returns agency to the user, allowing anyone with access to digital hardware and the internet to participate economically. These assets open new vistas of opportunity for economic empowerment and investment previously inaccessible due to excessive costs or daunting entry requirements.

Critics might point to the volatility of cryptocurrency as a deterrent, concerned about sudden price drops. However, stablecoins have emerged within the crypto ecosystem to address this issue, offering stable digital currencies pegged to traditional fiat money like the US Dollar or Euro. They hold the advantage of crypto's low transaction fees while providing a less volatile value, which allows users to enjoy cost benefits without enduring crippling instability.

As we disentangle these nuanced cost comparisons, it becomes evident that while there's no one-size-fits-all solution, the evolving landscape of cryptocurrency offers undeniable efficiency and cost benefits. These savings manifest not only in transactional fees but as broader financial liberation, particularly for those navigating stringent financial constraints or international differences.

Moving forward, our conversation will naturally pivot to these savings as facilitators of opportunity and inclusion. For the unbanked and underbanked, the lower costs of using cryptocurrencies can provide access in a way that traditional finance often struggles to equitably achieve. We'll explore how this financial accessibility is more than just a perk; it's a monumental step toward economic democratization for millions globally. These unfolding narratives present cryptocurrency not merely as an alternative but potentially as an equalizing force in the sphere of finance.

Opportunities for the Unbanked and Underbanked with New Financial Systems

In the previous section, we explored how transaction costs, service fees, and potential savings differ between crypto and traditional finance systems. These factors significantly impact users, especially those who are financially underserved. Reduced transaction costs and the potential for savings are leading more individuals to consider cryptocurrencies as a viable option. Now let's delve into how these cost benefits can create more accessible opportunities for the unbanked and underbanked populations.

Cryptocurrencies offer an unprecedented level of accessibility. Traditional banking systems often require documentation, credit history, and fees that many people simply cannot afford or access. In contrast, cryptocurrencies merely require an internet connection and a smartphone. This lowers the barriers significantly, allowing anyone from a street vendor in Nairobi to a remote farmer in Cambodia access to a global financial network. Blockchain technology, the backbone of cryptocurrencies, offers a degree of transparency and security that traditional financial systems struggle to match. Transactions are recorded on a public ledger, making fraud less likely while optimizing trust between parties.

Economic empowerment through cryptocurrencies manifests in various ways. For example, consider remittance payments. Traditionally, sending money cross-border involves significant fees and can take several days. Firms like Western Union charge hefty costs, eating into the funds that families receive. However, with cryptocurrencies such as Bitcoin or stablecoins like USDC, these transactions can be completed in seconds with a fraction of the fees. The impact on families receiving these funds is immediate. More money reaches its destination, providing better support for education, healthcare, and daily needs.

Additionally, cryptocurrencies empower individuals by democratizing access to capital. Traditional systems often require collateral or a credit score to issue loans. Cryptocurrencies leverage decentralized finance (DeFi) platforms to disrupt this norm. Imagine a small business owner in rural India looking to expand her shop. Without access to a bank, she struggles to get a loan. DeFi platforms, however, allow her to stake her crypto assets to receive a loan, bypassing the need for a lengthy credit check process. It fosters an environment where small businesses, often the lifelines of communities, can thrive without oppressive financial hurdles.

Participating in the global economy becomes a tangible reality through crypto adoption. Traditional finance often limits individuals to local economies, especially in developing regions. Cryptocurrencies break these geographical barriers. Take, for instance, freelancers or digital artists who can now easily offer their services worldwide and receive payments in cryptocurrencies. This not only increases their potential market size but also offers more competitive pricing globally. In Venezuela, where hyperinflation devalues local currency, freelancers have turned to cryptocurrencies like Bitcoin and Ethereum to stabilize their income and preserve wealth.

Anecdotal evidence sheds further light on how impactful cryptocurrencies have become. In Nigeria, where access to traditional financial systems is inconsistent and often unreliable, young entrepreneurs fuel a vibrant economy by opting for Bitcoin. They utilize crypto primarily for its stability compared to their national currency, the naira, which often fluctuates dramatically due to economic mismanagement. This shift empowers a new generation of business owners who can now engage confidently in business transactions, expand their reach, and safeguard their savings against local currency volatility.

Case studies from the unbanked populations in the Philippines show similar developments. Mobile apps have been developed that allow for direct cryptocurrency transactions without the need for a bank, providing real-time transfers that empower daily wage workers. For island communities where establishing physical bank branches is unfeasible, these digital solutions revolutionize financial interactions, offering a bridge over the digital divide with tangible, lasting impacts.

Cryptocurrencies promote financial literacy by fostering an environment where traditional financial norms are questioned and redefined. As individuals engage with digital currencies, they learn to navigate and understand financial markets, investments, and risk management independently. This newfound knowledge not only broadens

personal financial strategies but also fosters community-led educational programs. Initiatives in South African townships illustrate this, where blockchain workshops teach locals about financial independence through crypto. These initiatives offer long-term solutions that foster resilience against financial exclusion.
Despite these opportunities, the risks associated with cryptocurrencies are real and must be acknowledged. Market volatility, security loopholes, and regulatory uncertainties can pose significant challenges. However, ongoing developments in technology, along with a growing ecosystem of stablecoins and more secure platforms, attempt to address these concerns. Companies are increasingly focusing on building user-friendly interfaces aimed at minimizing risks for novice users.

Moreover, governments are beginning to recognize the potential that cryptocurrencies hold for economic empowerment and financial inclusion. Some regulators in emerging economies are setting frameworks aimed at protecting users while encouraging innovation in the crypto sector. El Salvador made global headlines as it adopted Bitcoin as legal tender, recognizing the potential to enhance financial inclusion. If implemented effectively, these policies could inspire similar actions in other nations and create a more inclusive global financial landscape.
Cryptocurrency innovation doesn't end here. Project-based models aim to integrate renewable energy projects with blockchain to offer energy credits in digital currency, addressing not only financial inclusion but also environmental challenges. Similarly, education-based models incentivize learning with crypto rewards, like GoodDollar, fostering a virtuous cycle of education and financial literacy.
As we analyze these facets, it becomes clear that cryptocurrencies provide a real pathway for financial empowerment for the unbanked and underbanked. They are more than just monetary tokens; they represent autonomy, inclusion, and potential. The financially underserved need not remain on the periphery, but rather, they can actively participate and thrive within an evolving digital economy. The challenge lies in bridging the information gap and tackling regulatory hurdles, but the potential rewards can redefine financial engagement for millions.

Bringing It All Together

As we conclude, the examination of accessibility, speed, and cost unveiled the vast potentials hidden within both cryptocurrency and traditional finance systems. For crypto newcomers and curious minds, understanding these contrasts shines a light on new avenues for financial inclusion and empowerment, especially for the unbanked and underbanked. Aspiring investors and entrepreneurs now glimpse possibilities for reducing costs while navigating faster, borderless transactions. The implications extend to policymakers and educators, who recognize crypto's promise in bridging economic gaps and transforming financial landscapes globally. Now armed with this knowledge, we can embrace an evolving future where digital currencies pave pathways toward broader financial freedom, encouraging innovative solutions that address the needs of diverse populations and drive inclusive economic growth.

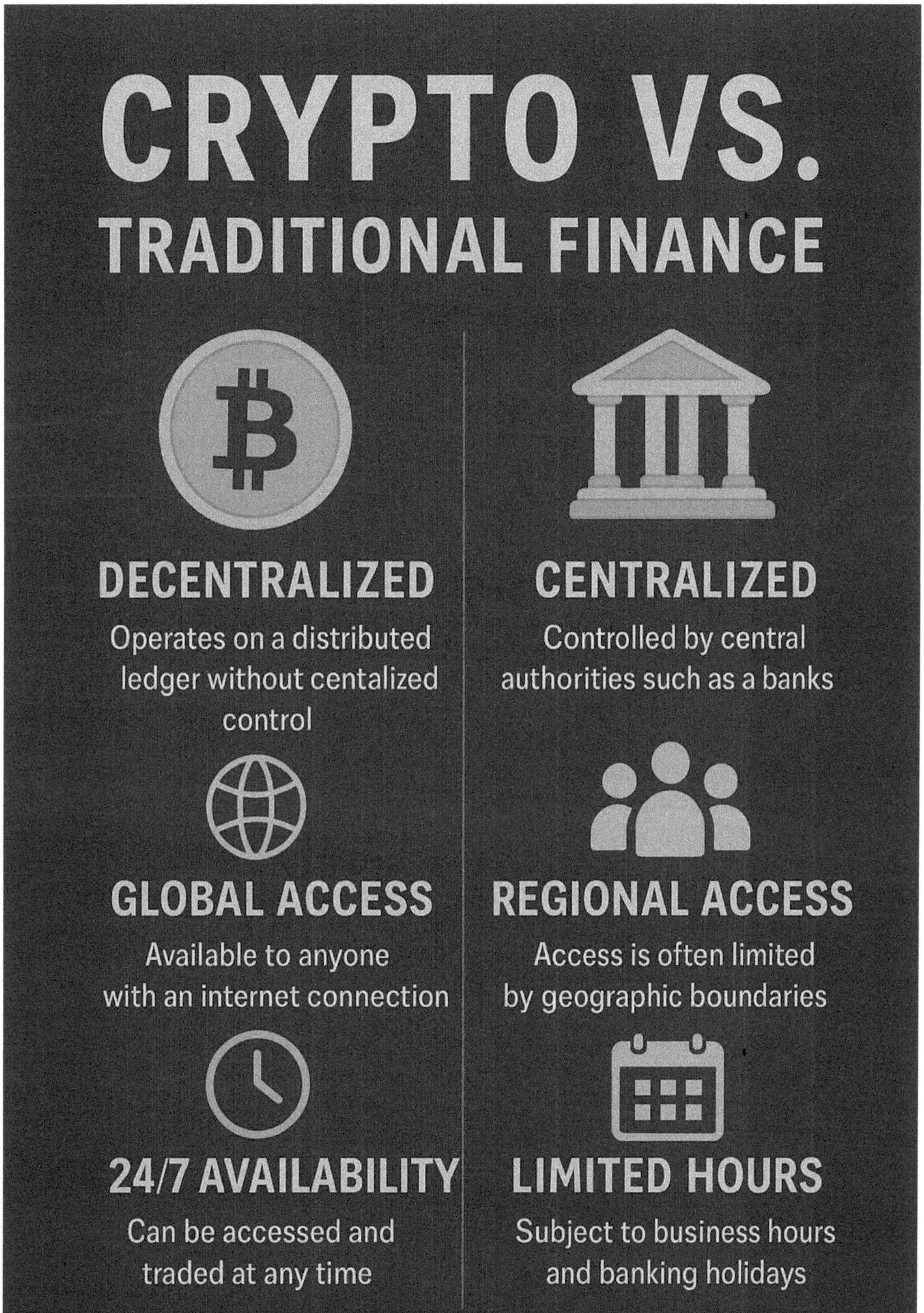
CRYPTO VS.
TRADITIONAL FINANCE
DECENTRALIZED
Operates on a distributed ledger without centalized control
CENTRALIZED
Controlled by central authorities such as a banks
GLOBAL ACCESS
Available to anyone with an internet connection
REGIONAL ACCESS
Access is often limited by geographic boundaries
24/7 AVAILABILITY
Can be accessed and traded at any time
LIMITED HOURS
Subject to business hours and banking holidays

Chapter 4: *Financial Inclusion for the Unbanked*

Financial Inclusion for the Unbanked

Ama, a resourceful tailor in Ghana, sat outside her small shop with piles of vibrant kente fabrics folded beside her. Despite her talent and ambition, her dreams of expanding her business were constantly thwarted by the traditional banking system. Without steady employment or a credit history, securing a loan was impossible, leaving her aspirations threadbare. Like many in her community, Ama was unbanked, trapped within financial systems that seemed designed to exclude her rather than offer support. Each day was a reminder of the limitations imposed by her lack of access to formal financial services, echoing a challenge faced across much of Africa.

Ama's story is all too common; millions like her find themselves on the fringes of financial inclusion. While the world speeds toward an interconnected future, many remain bound by outdated systems that fail to address their realities. This chapter will explore how cryptocurrency is reshaping financial accessibility, providing alternative avenues for empowerment and growth. By illuminating real stories from various communities, we will examine the revolutionary role digital currencies are playing in leveling the economic playing field globally.

Real Stories from Africa

In Ghana, a small business owner named Ama found herself constantly struggling against traditional banking systems that seemed to exclude her. Without formal employment or credit history, she was unable to secure loans to expand her small tailoring business. Like many others in her community, Ama was unbanked. Enter cryptocurrency, promising an alternative to conventional financial avenues. Ama began accepting payments via cryptocurrency, using her mobile phone to transact securely and efficiently, bypassing the need for a traditional bank account altogether. This newfound financial capability allowed her to expand her business, hire more tailors, and cater to a growing number of customers. Her story is one of many illustrating how cryptocurrency technologies can empower individuals otherwise marginalized by traditional financial systems.

In Nigeria, the story echoes a similar theme. The country, known for its entrepreneurial zeal, is fertile ground for digital innovation. With a significant percentage of the population lacking access to formal banking services, cryptocurrencies have become the key to financial inclusion. Here, digital currencies like Bitcoin and Ethereum aren't just speculative assets; they represent legitimate currencies used to conduct day-to-day transactions. From buying groceries to paying for education, Nigerians are using cryptocurrencies to overcome the hurdles presented by cash shortages and banking inefficiencies. In rural areas, where physical banks are few and far between, mobile access to cryptocurrencies is bridging geographical barriers and empowering individuals to engage in the economy in ways they never could before.

Such developments are not without challenges. In Kenya, for instance, a vibrant case study shows both the potential and the complexities of adopting cryptocurrency. While the government explores regulating and providing a framework for cryptocurrencies, many Kenyans have already embraced them. The widespread use of mobile money, such as M-Pesa, has primed the nation for digital currency adoption. Many individuals use cryptocurrencies to facilitate cross-border remittances, which are often plagued by hefty fees through traditional channels. This process is particularly important for families relying on remittances from overseas workers. By using digital currencies, they can avoid high transaction fees and receive funds instantly, offering them a more reliable means of support.

Education has become a crucial factor in propelling cryptocurrency adoption. In Uganda, various non-profits and technology companies have embarked on educational campaigns to inform citizens about the benefits and risks of digital currencies. Workshops underscore the technology behind cryptocurrencies, focusing on security and practical applications while demystifying the subject for regular people. These initiatives are critical because, without understanding, mass adoption remains a dream rather than a reality. This emphasis on education empowers more Ugandans to dip their toes into the world of digital finance, fostering the ability to make informed decisions and actively participate in the local economy.

In South Africa, cryptocurrency's role extends to solving issues of economic disparity. Here, some informal settlements are using blockchain technology to create community currencies which are built on cryptocurrency platforms. These local currencies help stimulate community-based trade by keeping resources circulating within the neighborhood. They also mitigate risks associated with cash theft and fraud. For people living in vulnerable areas, digital currencies provide not only a means of financial participation but also a newfound sense of economic control.

Moreover, traditional banking systems often exclude women disproportionately in many African countries. Cryptocurrency is slowly changing this narrative by offering women more control over their financial resources. In rural Zimbabwe, some women have taken to using Bitcoin to save money spread across secure, digital wallets, giving them a safe space to manage their finances independently. This empowerment has led to increased entrepreneurship among women, contributing to the financial health and stability of their families and communities.

Critics might say that cryptocurrencies only serve a niche audience, but evidence from African markets suggests otherwise. The flexibility and ease of use that cryptocurrencies offer are overcoming deeply rooted financial obstacles. They are increasing access to goods and services in new, innovative ways. For instance, farmers in Ethiopia are beginning to utilize blockchain technology for supply chain management. Cryptocurrencies can provide documentation and verification of transactions, reducing corruption and ensuring that farmers receive fair payment for their products.

In Madagascar, where internet penetration is gradually improving, digital currencies offer an opportunity to leapfrog traditional banking systems. Startups in the region are exploring how cryptocurrency can be integrated into everyday commerce, expanding financial access rapidly. Although infrastructural challenges remain, there is excitement about what the digital revolution can bring.

The ongoing digital transformation extends beyond transactions to include the potential of cryptocurrency in creating new avenues for investment. In Senegal, entrepreneurs are exploring Initial Coin Offerings (ICOs) as an alternative means of fundraising. This shift not only democratizes access to investment opportunities but also fosters innovation in technology and business sectors previously starved of capital.

The versatility of digital currencies, from facilitating everyday transactions to offering investment possibilities, is reshaping Africa's financial landscape. By providing secure and affordable access to financial services, cryptocurrencies are bridging the gap for millions.

As we turn our attention to Asia, we find different yet equally inspiring stories of cryptocurrency adoption. In countries like the Philippines and Indonesia, digital currencies are transforming access to financial services, mirroring and expanding the pioneering efforts we see across Africa.

Real Stories from Asia

Drawing from the narratives in African nations, where cryptocurrency has reimagined borders in financial inclusion, the shift heads eastward towards Asia. In countries where traditional banking infrastructures remain sporadic or inaccessible, cryptocurrencies have risen as a potent alternative. Look at Indonesia, where a large segment of the population remains unbanked. Many individuals here rely heavily on cash transactions, which limits their participation in broader financial activities. Cryptocurrency emerges as a bridge, creating a digital economy where previously none existed.

Consider the experience in India, another technology-driven nation with a significant unbanked population. The country has a burgeoning digital payments sector, already replete with mobile applications and fintech innovations. Yet, despite these advancements, a significant number of people outside urban centers still face financial barriers. Cryptocurrency solutions offer a lifeline, providing these populations with secure, transparent, and cost-effective financial instruments. Rural entrepreneurs can now engage with global markets, sell products abroad, and receive payments in digital currencies with transparency and security, all without requiring a conventional bank account.

Meanwhile, in the Philippines, remittances form a critical economic pillar. Overseas workers often face exorbitant fees and delays in sending money home. By embracing blockchain-based solutions, remittances have become faster and substantially cheaper, revolutionizing how earnings flow back to their home country. This shift bolsters not just the individual households receiving funds but also the broader national economy, as remittance fees shrink and efficiency increases.

A closer look at Vietnam reveals an intriguing trend where digital currency uptake is accelerating, driven primarily by tech-savvy younger generations. These individuals, often underserved by traditional financial systems, are bypassing traditional banking methods entirely, choosing instead to utilize crypto-wallets for savings, investments, and daily transactions. This burgeoning movement showcases how digital advancements are fostering financial independence, especially among young entrepreneurs and startups that now find it viable to expand product offerings and outreach without infrastructural constraints.

In China, although the regulatory environment around cryptocurrencies remains somewhat restrictive, the public's appetite for blockchain technology is immense. Innovators and entrepreneurs are exploring new avenues to integrate digital currencies within existing e-commerce ecosystems, potentially revolutionizing how transactions occur on platforms like Alibaba and JD.com. Their approach highlights how digital currencies could seamlessly support already established digital payment systems, potentially reaching pockets of the country where financial inclusion remains limited.

Japan presents a different narrative yet equally compelling. The country's receptiveness to technology and innovation positions it as a leader in cryptocurrency adoption. Regulatory frameworks, considered one of the most comprehensive globally, provide a stable environment conducive to growth and innovation. Everyday transactions, from buying groceries to booking travel, increasingly occur using digital currencies. The Japanese experience illustrates how clear guidance and proactive regulations can nurture a digital economy intertwined with everyday life, promoting accessibility to all economic demographics.

Flying back down to the island of Sri Lanka, where local entrepreneurs have begun harnessing digital currencies to overcome economic uncertainties. Cryptocurrencies offer them access to stable global currencies, safeguarding savings from local currency fluctuations. This financial resilience is critical as communities recover from economic downturns, allowing them to build back stronger by investing in education, healthcare, and entrepreneurial ventures independent of volatile traditional economic systems.

The focus slightly shifts when observing Hong Kong, a major financial hub with deep ties to international markets. Here, cryptocurrencies demonstrate an alternative asset class, broadening investment portfolios and providing more channels for wealth growth. Residents harness blockchain for diverse financial activities, from property transactions to stock market trades, revealing the island's integration of digital currency into the fabric of its financial services.

Bangladesh offers another transformative example. Farmers in remote areas, previously isolated from mainstream financial transactions, now receive fair prices for their goods through blockchain-led initiatives. Cryptocurrencies eliminate the middlemen in these transactions, offering a cooperative model of trade where transparency and fair pricing prevail, reshaping the economic landscape for rural communities.

These varied stories highlight a regional trend where cryptocurrencies not only enhance accessibility but deeply embed themselves into the economic activities of everyday life. By fostering financial inclusion, they invite more individuals into the financial fold, democratizing opportunities previously reserved for those connected to formal banking avenues.

Our narrative builds anticipation for the exploration of Latin American examples, where cryptocurrencies also pave new pathways towards financial invisibility. Looking at upcoming innovations unfolding, it's evident that the digital currency revolution holds unique local nuances, yet shares a universal vision: to provide accessible, efficient, and equitable financial services for all.

Real Stories from Latin America

The previous section delved into success stories from Asian regions, showing how digital currencies have transformed financial services. It demonstrated significant changes that open new doors for communities that traditionally lacked banking access. Building on this narrative, attention now turns to Latin America, where transformations through cryptocurrency are making strides in promoting financial inclusion.

Latin America provides a fascinating study in crypto's ability to enhance financial accessibility. Consider El Salvador, which has taken a bold leap by adopting Bitcoin as legal tender. Half of the country's population did not have access to traditional financial services, yet with Bitcoin, they can bypass banking formalities, directly engaging in commerce through digital wallets. This shift presents individuals and small businesses

with opportunities for growth previously hindered by costly remittance fees and the absence of bank branches.
Brazil offers another example where crypto's reach is felt. With some areas suffering from economic instability and high inflation, cryptocurrencies present a haven from the devaluation of local currency. Paxos and Mercado Bitcoin, prominent crypto platforms, contribute by providing cheap and secure transactions, granting many the opportunity to save and invest without the traditional financial institution headaches. This access stands out, especially for those living in rural regions where banks are scarce, but smartphones are not.
Imagine a craftsman in Paraguay who sells products online. Traditionally, cross-border sales would involve a labyrinth of paperwork and banking transactions. Now, through crypto exchanges tailored for low transaction costs, this craftsman can reach international customers more efficiently. He uses digital currencies as a medium, avoiding hefty fees and delays, effectively expanding his business prospects beyond the local market.
Another area ripe for transformation is remittances. Millions of Latin Americans depend on money sent from relatives abroad. Typically, receiving these funds involves exorbitant transfer fees, cutting into the amount that the family gets back home. Bitso, a Mexican cryptocurrency exchange, is transformative by enabling quicker, cheaper remittance options directly between relatives, streamlining what was once a cumbersome process. Not only does this service highlight the economic benefits, but it also fosters a sense of security for families knowing they can access much-needed funds easily.

Cryptocurrencies also play a role in empowering the unbanked population in countries like Venezuela. Faced with hyperinflation, traditional banking solutions offer little refuge. Digital currencies provide an alternative path to financial stability. By swapping rapidly depreciating local currency for stablecoins, individuals maintain their purchasing power. This strategy, while not without its challenges, exemplifies an innovative approach to dealing with economic hardships.
Look further at Argentina, where grassroots organizations use cryptocurrency to foster microloans. Thanks to lower interest rates and the elimination of intermediaries, individuals gain access to much-needed capital. These microloans are practical for entrepreneurs looking to start small ventures or farmers needing investment. The absence of traditional banking hurdles nurtures a culture of entrepreneurship and proliferates economic opportunities within these communities.
Each example highlights a mechanism—currency stability in Brazil, international commerce from Paraguay, remittance channels in Mexico, or microloans in Argentina—illustrating crypto's malleable solutions. By bypassing conventional banking inadequacies, these avenues expand financial inclusion in a tangible, sustainable manner. The digital currency ecosystem offers a lifeline in regions where economic challenges are a daily reality, reinventing the approach to financial solutions and augmenting economic opportunities at the grassroots level.

Moreover, crypto's transparency and reduced potential for corruption resonate in countries plagued by mistrust in financial systems. Blockchain's distributed ledger presents a trustworthy alternative, promoting accountability and restoring faith in monetary exchanges—a critical factor for regions with limited financial infrastructure.

Of course, challenges remain. Cryptocurrency adoption requires educational initiatives to ensure individuals understand how to manage digital assets securely. Governments wrestling with regulatory frameworks must find a balance that encourages innovation while protecting consumers. People must navigate potential volatility, highlighting the necessity of evolving and adaptive strategies. However, these hurdles are not insurmountable and point toward robust engagement and collaboration between the technology sector, consumers, and governments.

As the focus continues to mobile wallets and their growing role in financial transactions, they offer another promising element for expanding crypto's reach. These tools enable seamless currency exchanges and secure storage solutions, further dissolving traditional barriers. By ensuring anyone with mobile connectivity can access financial services, mobile wallets hold the potential to extend crypto's benefits globally.

Cryptocurrency's role in broadening access to financial services finds substantial proof in its impact throughout Latin America. Every community within these regions presents unique conditions for innovation, allowing crypto to adapt and expand its utility in novel ways. The transformations that digital currencies nurture are ongoing, with promising signs that adaptability and collaboration will continue driving this momentum. As the narrative moves forward, mobile wallets promise to erase boundaries even further, ensuring financial inclusion continues to evolve from aspiration to reality.

Introduction to Mobile Wallets

In previous discussions, we explored how Latin American communities have embraced innovative financial tools to improve access and inclusion. Mobile wallets, for instance, have become game-changers in expanding opportunities for those who historically lacked access to traditional banking services. We see examples of how people in these regions leverage technology to facilitate daily financial transactions, leading us into a comprehensive understanding of mobile wallets and their global significance.

Mobile wallets are digital applications that store payment card information on mobile devices, effectively turning your smartphone into a bank card. Their practical aspects are simple yet revolutionary, involving the ability to store, send, and receive money digitally. This flexibility offers users the ease of financial management at their fingertips, without the need for a traditional bank account. With the rise of smartphones globally, mobile wallets have taken root even in remote and underserved areas, bringing a semblance of financial independence.

Functions of mobile wallets are crucial; they allow instantaneous transactions without the physical exchange of money or visits to a bank—a boon in areas where banking infrastructure is undeveloped or nonexistent. For instance, in Africa, where many regions struggle with sparse banking facilities, mobile wallet services like M-Pesa have effectively bypassed these barriers. This system allows users to deposit, withdraw, transfer money, and pay for goods and services using only mobile phones. Such platforms redefine financial access, bridging gaps that physical banks cannot—due to geographical, infrastructural, or economic constraints.

Globally, mobile wallets exemplify a shift towards digital currency, making them indispensable for industry workers, small business owners, and everyday consumers who need easy access to financial services. In regions like Southeast Asia, mobile wallet usage is burgeoning due to its simplicity and adaptability to local economies. Here, small merchants use them to accept payments directly from customers' phones,

sidestepping the need for costly card reader systems. This not only streamlines business operations but also attracts more customers who prefer quick and cashless transactions.
The impact of mobile wallets extends beyond individuals to entire communities, fostering inclusion by reducing transaction costs and removing the need for a physical bank visit. As mobile service coverage extends into rural areas, digital financial services follow, offering inexpensive and accessible options. This spurs economic activity, as more people participate in the digital economy, creating ripple effects that benefit the broader market.

Grasping the significance of mobile wallets requires examining their role in digital currency. They serve as gateways to cryptographic currencies, offering functions that fiat currencies alone may not support. Here, barriers like currency exchange fees or delays in international money transfers are often mitigated, allowing seamless transactions. This access happens in real-time, providing users with up-to-date financial control. By public adoption of such technologies, the path to inclusive finance becomes less hindered by geographical or economic obstacles.
Concrete implementations showcase mobile wallets' success in elevating financial inclusion. In Kenya, for instance, the M-Pesa system allows users to manage funds without a traditional bank account. Similarly, India's Unified Payments Interface (UPI) transforms smartphones into full-fledged financial instruments. Rather than stand in bank lines, users can transfer money, pay utility bills, or conduct business transactions from anywhere, anytime. Such systems not only reduce transaction times but also costs, an essential factor in attracting unbanked users.

Mobile wallets also offer security benefits. Encryption and authentication features protect user data and transactions, thereby gaining trust and encouraging broader usage. Though concerns about cybersecurity remain, the reinforcement of digital security protocols ensures these platforms continue to be safe and reliable.
Another strong example lies in Latin America, where the use of mobile wallets in countries like Brazil showcases how entire economies benefit. The emphasis on mobile technology has spurred growth in e-commerce, with more retailers accepting digital payments. This inclusion is vital for those without bank accounts, as mobile wallets provide an accessible entry into the online economy, broadening their consumer base and economic influence.
By facilitating easier and cheaper access to digital finance, mobile wallets empower users to partake in economic activities beyond their national borders. Financial inclusion gained here aids in stabilizing economies, particularly in regions experiencing economic uncertainty. For most, these wallets serve as their first introduction to formal financial systems, teaching fiscal management and literacy through use.
Ultimately, the adaptive nature of mobile wallets speaks to their potential in turning financial inclusion initiatives into tangible realities. They democratize finance by offering everyone, regardless of socio-economic status, the ability to partake in the digital economy. Looking forward, the transition from traditional financial systems to those based on mobile wallets establishes a solid foundation for future innovations, such as microtransactions.

The paths made possible by mobile wallets set the stage for smaller, frequent financial engagements that cater to low-income users. As we explore microtransactions next, understand how these tiny transactions unlock everyday financial potential—thanks in large part to the accessibility that mobile wallets provide. It's this nexus of technology and finance that hones a focus on empowering individuals with limited resources, ensuring they have the tools needed for their financial journey.

Microtransactions and Their Significance

Microtransactions, tiny yet potent financial actions, wear the cape of the everyday hero for those in underserved areas. Picture a street vendor in Nairobi, using her mobile phone to process small payments from her customers, each one too small to engage with through traditional banking systems. This dance of digital currency isn't just about convenience. It's about financial empowerment, an essential tool for those without conventional bank accounts to engage with the modern economy.

Consider the vast expanse of rural India, where the nearest bank branch might involve a journey of hours, if not days. Here, microtransactions via mobile wallets enable everyday purchases and savings previously complicated by the distance. When you're living on a few dollars a day, being able to carry your "bank" in your pocket empowers you to save, spend, and secure your financial future. Such micro-leaps, although small in isolation, can compound to significant economic milestones.

In the heart of bustling Lagos, microtransactions play out as a socio-economic symphony. They reduce the high transaction costs historically associated with accessing small amounts of capital. Typically, high fees have acted as a gatekeeper, barring many from engaging in essential financial activities. But now, families can transfer small sums to one another with ease, fueling everyday expenses or emergencies without the pressing concern of exorbitant fees. This reduction in transaction cost is game-changing, particularly in extending financial services to populations that need it most.

Microtransactions also weave into the daily fabric of life in parts of Southeast Asia, where street vendors and small businesses have traditionally relied on cash. Here, the transition to digital currency enables even the smallest of purchases, like a single piece of fruit or a spicy skewered snack, to be made without cash changing hands. These digital exchanges integrate unbanked individuals into broader economic networks and break down barriers that cash-oriented cultures have long observed.

Access to microtransactions doesn't just alter day-to-day financial interactions; it opens new doorways for community development. In regions like Latin America, communal savings groups—small cooperatives of neighbors pooling resources for mutual benefit—flourish under the low-transaction cost banner of micro-financing. These groups use digital platforms to collect, manage, and distribute funds. This grassroots level of engagement shows a profound shift towards inclusivity, where communities are no longer financially isolated islands but part of a larger economic archipelago.

What's exciting about microtransactions is not only their increasing ubiquity but their role in democratizing finance. Suppose you're a farm worker in rural Peru turning a few soles into micro-investments. With them, you can access e-learning platforms, purchase seeds during off-seasons, or invest in solar chargers for your home. These not only improve individual livelihoods but uplift entire communities. The ripple effect is measurable. As individuals achieve greater financial stability, they spend more locally, small businesses thrive, and communities can invest in infrastructure improvements—they are more likely to reinvest in services like education and community health.

Take the example of microtransactions facilitating access to solar power solutions in a small Kenyan village. Here, families use mobile payments to acquire solar chargers for their homes—an upfront purchase that proved financially impossible without a payment plan broken down into microtransactions. These transactions allow even the smallest financial contributions to accumulate towards a larger goal: light. As homes light up, children can study at night, businesses operate longer, and households save on traditional fuel expenses.

Furthermore, the reduction in transaction costs, achieved through microtransactions, can't be overstated. No longer does sending money across localities or borders require forfeiting a large percentage as fees. This fact alone has shifted family dynamics, enabling workers abroad to support loved ones back home with less friction. The emotional and financial burden eases, lending toward more significant financial literacy and security as families budget and plan without fear of hidden costs evaporating their earnings.

Microtransactions' role in fostering economic inclusivity is profound in fostering entrepreneurship among women. In the Middle East, women leverage small, consistent investments to grow side businesses into reliable income sources. Their tales aren't just success stories; they exemplify how micro-lending, once too cumbersome for traditional banking structures, is revitalizing entire sectors of the population. These financial actions accumulate, unfettered by large fees or the necessity of a physical presence at a bank.

The impact of technology, as a facilitator for these transactions, speaks volumes about its promise for deeper financial access. One cannot ignore the liberating feeling of autonomy and agency it brings to the unbanked. With each tap and click, there's a feeling that financial systems once impenetrable are now opening up, a vault unlocked by the very same economy it serves.

Real change stems from the ground up, and microtransactions fuel this transformative fire in everyday life. They are not just about currency changes but represent shifting attitudes towards what it means to be economically active. They illustrate how, by stringing together micro-actions, we can weave a grand economic tapestry which practices inclusion and provides opportunities that were previously unimaginable. As technology evolves and expands its reach, it serves as a reminder of how we can build resilient economies, not just for some, but for all.

Conclusion

As we've explored, the role of cryptocurrency in enhancing financial accessibility globally is both transformative and essential. From small business owners in Ghana to tech-savvy youth in Vietnam, digital currencies are reshaping how people engage with the economy, bypassing the limitations of traditional banking systems. These powerful narratives demonstrate that cryptocurrency offers more than just a new kind of money—it provides empowerment, independence, and opportunity for those often marginalized by conventional financial infrastructures. Now that we understand the potential of these digital assets, we can work towards integrating them further into our economies, fostering global financial inclusion and creating a future where everyone has access to the financial tools they need to thrive. This ongoing digital revolution promises a world where borders fade and financial empowerment becomes a universal reality.

FINANCIAL INCLUSION FOR THE UNBANKED

BRIDGING THE FINANCIAL GAP

ACCESS TO FINANCIAL SERVICES

Cryptocurrency provides an alternative for those without bank accounts

CROSS-BORDER TRANSACTIONS

Enables fast, low-cost international money transfers

ECONOMIC EMPOWERMENT

Allows individuals to save, invest, and secure their finances

FINANCIAL LITERACY

Promotes education and awareness of managing digital assets

Chapter 5: *Empowering Entrepreneurs and Small Businesses*

Empowering Entrepreneurs and Small Businesses

In a bustling market in Nairobi, tech entrepreneur Aisha stood by her small booth and pondered the future of her fledgling startup. She had an incredible idea that could revolutionize water quality monitoring, but access to traditional funding avenues was elusive. High-interest loans and long approval times loomed as insurmountable hurdles. Meanwhile, across the ocean, small business owners like Santiago in Colombia faced similar challenges. The staggering costs and extended delays involved in receiving international payments felt like heavy chains pulling back their dreams. Small enterprises worldwide share these tales. Entrepreneurs are stifled not by the lack of innovation but by limited financial opportunities.

The rise of cryptocurrencies is challenging the status quo, offering new solutions where barriers seemed impermeable. In this chapter, we delve into how crowdfunding, remittances, and cross-border trade are being transformed through cryptocurrencies, providing entrepreneurs and small businesses unprecedented opportunities for growth on a global stage.

Crowdfunding

Cryptocurrency's impact on crowdfunding opens exciting paths for entrepreneurs seeking streamlined access to capital. Unlike traditional funding methods that often come with barriers such as high fees and lengthy approval processes, crypto-based platforms present a democratized alternative. These digital currencies allow startups to tap into a global pool of investors, transcending geographical limitations and financial barriers that can stifle innovation.

Consider the case of a tech startup in Nairobi utilizing cryptocurrency to fund an innovative project aimed at improving water quality. By launching a crypto-based crowdfunding campaign, this startup could access funds from supporters worldwide without the constraints of conventional banking systems. This approach not only speeds up the funding process but also connects the startup with backers who are genuinely interested in the venture, not just the potential financial returns. This illustrates one of the key advantages of cryptocurrency in crowdfunding—it fosters a community of engaged supporters who believe in the core mission and technology driving the project.

Creating a successful crypto crowdfunding campaign involves several critical steps. First, a business must choose a suitable cryptocurrency platform that aligns with its goals. Platforms like Ethereum enable users to create custom tokens, which represent a stake or reward in the project, providing investors with tangible benefits tied to their financial contribution. Once a platform is selected, careful planning is necessary to define the project's goals, timeline, and funding needs. Detailed transparency regarding how the funds will be used is crucial; this builds trust and assures potential investors of the project's legitimacy and viability.

After setting a clear path, businesses should focus on maximizing visibility. Due to the borderless nature of cryptocurrencies, effective digital marketing can propel a campaign into the global spotlight. Engaging storytelling can resonate with a diverse investor base, amplifying the reach and attractiveness of the fundraising effort. Furthermore, employing social media strategies and leveraging influencers within the space can significantly drive investor interest and participation, transforming a local initiative into an international success story.

Challenges, of course, exist in the realm of cryptocurrency crowdfunding. One such obstacle is the volatility inherent in digital currencies. Drastic price fluctuations can either significantly benefit or harm both startups and investors. Addressing this requires crafting a stable fundraising plan and setting safeguard measures like pegging raised funds to stablecoins, which maintain value better than traditional cryptocurrencies. Also, regulatory uncertainty poses a significant challenge. In some jurisdictions, the legal framework governing cryptocurrency remains undefined or continuously evolving, which can discourage potential investors wary of compliance issues. Startups must stay informed of regulations within their countries and those where their potential investors reside. Consulting with legal experts to ensure adherence to international financial laws can mitigate fears over compliance, enhancing investor confidence.

Notwithstanding these challenges, the benefits of crypto-based crowdfunding often dwarf the perceived setbacks. Traditional platforms can impose significant fees, sometimes absorbing a notable percentage of the funds raised. Cryptocurrency transactions, in contrast, often carry lower fees, enabling entrepreneurs to allocate a larger portion of the raised capital directly toward project development and execution. This efficiency makes it easier for startups to bring their visions to fruition without shrinking their budget due to overhead costs.

The global nature of cryptocurrency also imbues a distinctive sense of community among backers. Enterprises often cultivate relationships with their funders beyond simple transactions. In many cases, investors can become brand advocates, participating in decision-making or providing skills and insights that guide project growth. These interactions can create a feedback loop, ensuring projects evolve in ways that meet backer expectations and market demands.

As businesses grow, this cyclical dynamic fosters a symbiotic relationship between entrepreneurs and their investors, inciting long-term success for both parties. The transparency of blockchain, a core element of cryptocurrency, allows all transactions and project developments to be tracked publicly. This open-accounting framework alleviates investor concerns about mismanagement or fraud, critical components for establishing a trustworthy funding environment where accountability thrives.

The transition to traditional banking is seamless for businesses leveraging crypto funding. Many enterprises, after achieving funding goals, choose to convert their cryptocurrency into fiat, enabling broader operational activities, such as paying local suppliers or employees. This hybrid approach ensures that while startups initially leverage the disruptive benefits of cryptocurrency, they can still integrate smoothly into existing financial systems as their operations scale.

In closing this exploration of crowdfunding, we acknowledge how cryptocurrencies uniquely empower small businesses to achieve complex objectives unfettered by geographic confines or traditional gateway constraints. These platforms not only unlock opportunities for invention and expansion but also cultivate a new era of financial

interaction defined by inclusivity and transparency.
Moving forward, we'll see how cryptocurrencies impact remittances, another crucial area of importance for small businesses maneuvering through the global landscape. By reducing transaction costs and mitigating time delays, digital currencies present real advantages for companies reliant on international payments and fund transfers, further leveling the playing field for businesses seeking growth in a competitive global market.

Remittances

Cryptocurrencies have revolutionized crowdfunding by enabling seamless global access to investors. This system provides a launching pad for discussing how cryptocurrencies similarly enhance the remittance process. Just as entrepreneurs benefit from globally accessible crowdfunding, they also navigate a streamlined remittance landscape. Cryptocurrencies play a transformative role by addressing key inefficiencies that traditionally plague international money transfers.
The traditional remittance landscape, dominated by banks and established service providers, often imposes significant barriers. These include high transaction costs, prolonged processing times, and limited access, especially for small businesses. Cryptocurrencies break down these walls, offering a more efficient and cost-effective alternative. They eliminate the need for intermediaries, slashing transaction fees and alleviating the burden of excessive financial charges. For small businesses operating on tight margins, this cost reduction makes a noticeable impact, enabling more funds to be re-invested into operations and growth.

Cryptocurrencies facilitate instant transactions. Unlike conventional systems where cross-border payments can take several days, crypto transactions typically settle within minutes. This speed is particularly valuable in managing cash flow for businesses that rely on timely payments to sustain operations. A smoother cash flow process enhances a small business's ability to manage inventory, pay suppliers promptly, and seize new opportunities without financial hesitation.
Consider the example of an entrepreneur in a developing country who utilizes cryptocurrency to receive payments from international clients. This approach circumvents bureaucratic hurdles often associated with traditional banking systems. With crypto, she gains immediate access to her funds, allowing her to reinvest in her business, pay employees on time, and expand her network of suppliers. Ultimately, this facilitates not only business continuity but also growth.
A specific case involves a small textile business in Bangladesh. In the past, receiving international payments through standard channels was both time-consuming and costly due to high banking fees and currency conversion charges. The business owner switched to accepting payments in Bitcoin. This decision led to a 75% reduction in transaction costs and virtually eliminated the waiting period for funds. Other business owners facing similar challenges can learn from this example, considering the switch to cryptocurrency to benefit from similar efficiencies.

Another instance is a tech startup in Kenya, providing digital solutions to clients across the globe. The founder discovered that leveraging cryptocurrencies enabled him to bypass lengthy and expensive transactions typical of existing financial systems. This newfound efficiency empowered him to compete with larger companies, ultimately securing more international contracts and setting the foundation for rapid business growth.

While the benefits are clear, it's important to acknowledge that the transition to cryptocurrency comes with its own set of challenges. Volatility remains a significant concern for businesses, as currency values can fluctuate dramatically within short periods. However, stablecoins, which are pegged to traditional currencies, present a solution. They offer the benefits of cryptocurrencies without the volatility, making them a safe option for businesses looking to maintain value stability while transacting internationally.

Transparency, another feature of cryptocurrencies, also instills trust. The blockchain technology underpinning these digital currencies records each transaction on a public ledger. This visibility reduces the risk of fraud, disputes, and corruption often associated with cross-border payments. Businesses can track their funds in real time, providing peace of mind to both parties in a transaction.

As we look to the future, regulations around cryptocurrencies will continue to evolve. Governments worldwide are slowly adapting legal frameworks to accommodate this new financial landscape. This adaptation will hopefully bring about more stability and security, encouraging wider adoption among small businesses. Still, entrepreneurs and small business owners must remain informed about regulatory changes to ensure compliance and protect their investments.

The shift towards cryptocurrencies signals a growing recognition of their potential to simplify complex financial interactions. For small businesses accustomed to navigating numerous obstacles within traditional systems, this shift offers a fresh perspective. They gain access to a suite of financial tools that not only support current needs but also pave the way for future innovations.

The impact of cryptocurrencies extends beyond remittance efficiencies, setting a precedent for their role in facilitating cross-border trade, which we will explore in the next section. The same principles that reduce costs and expedite transactions similarly aid businesses in mitigating currency exchange issues. Cryptocurrencies minimize risks related to currency fluctuations, offering stability and security. Such advancements, coupled with the ability to track transactions accurately, make cryptocurrencies an attractive option for businesses venturing into global markets.

This analysis of remittances underscores cryptocurrency's ability to empower entrepreneurs, proving that these digital currencies offer more than just an alternative to traditional payment systems. They provide a gateway to a more inclusive, responsive, and transparent financial ecosystem. As we continue exploring, we see how these benefits extend to other facets of international business, upholding the promise of cryptocurrencies to reshape economic landscapes for small businesses worldwide.

Cross-border Trade

In the previous section, we examined how cryptocurrencies have transformed the field of remittances by reducing transaction costs and speeding up money transfers. These same benefits extend to cross-border trade, facilitating smoother international interactions. Traditional systems often grapple with high fees and lengthy delays which can hinder business operations, especially for small and medium-sized enterprises (SMEs). Cryptocurrencies, on the other hand, bypass these hurdles by providing a fast and cost-effective alternative to traditional trade methods. This is largely because digital currencies are decentralized, eliminating the need for financial intermediaries and enabling direct transfers between parties. Therefore, companies engaging in cross-

border trade can significantly lower operational costs.
Additionally, cryptocurrencies address currency exchange issues that might affect international sales. In a conventional trade environment, businesses must often navigate the complexities of fluctuating exchange rates. Such uncertainty can impact pricing strategies and profitability. Cryptocurrencies offer a solution by enabling transactions in a single digital currency, eliminating the need for currency conversion and the associated risks. This seamless approach allows businesses to operate with greater predictability and transparency, making it easier to plan for the long-term and manage financial expectations.

Fraud risks present another challenge in cross-border trade, particularly for smaller entities less equipped to absorb financial losses or legal battles. Cryptocurrencies help mitigate these risks through blockchain technology. Each transaction is verified and recorded on a decentralized ledger, ensuring transparency and immutability. This reduces the possibility of fraud or disputes as every transaction can be traced and authenticated with ease. For SMEs, this security measure can be particularly reassuring, as it fosters a safer environment for international transactions and builds trust between trading partners.
To illustrate these benefits in action, consider a small textiles company in India exporting goods to a retailer in Europe. Using traditional banking methods, they might face hefty transaction fees and a waiting period of several days for payments to clear. Fluctuating currency exchange rates could further complicate their pricing strategy. However, by accepting payments in cryptocurrencies like Bitcoin or Ethereum, the company can reduce transaction costs to a fraction of traditional fees and receive payments almost instantly. Moreover, conducting business in a stable digital currency circumvents the unpredictability of exchange rates entirely. This allows the textile company to maintain competitive pricing and reinvest savings into expanding their product lines or improving operations.

Another example is a tech startup in Kenya that provides software solutions to clients worldwide. Traditionally, they would have had to establish relationships with multiple banks and navigate complex international banking regulations to receive payments. This often results in slow transactions and difficulties in accessing funds. By integrating cryptocurrency payments, the startup can receive payments from anywhere in the world without the complications of banking bureaucracy. This direct payment process enhances cash flow management, enabling the startup to focus more resources on innovation and growth.
On a larger scale, multinational corporations are also adopting cryptocurrencies for their cross-border transactions, evidencing scalability and practicality for SMEs. For example, a corporation might use cryptocurrencies to simplify its supply chain payments, ensuring timely payments to suppliers spread across various countries. This not only ensures a smoother flow of goods but can also strengthen supplier relationships by consistently meeting payment commitments.

In addition to practical benefits, cryptocurrencies can also open new growth avenues for SMEs. By reducing cost barriers and facilitating easier international trade, small businesses can access new markets previously considered financially prohibitive. Digital currencies democratize international business, allowing even the smallest company to compete on a global scale. Businesses can now sell directly to international

consumers, simplifying the process and enhancing customer satisfaction due to lower costs and faster delivery.
Finally, the environmental impact of cryptocurrencies is an ongoing discussion, with some digital currencies attempting to reduce their carbon footprint. Efforts to make blockchain technology more sustainable offer promising prospects for SMEs concerned about environmental impact. By engaging with cryptocurrencies keen on sustainability, businesses can align themselves with environmentally responsible practices, appealing to like-minded consumers who prioritize eco-friendly business operations.
Having explored how cryptocurrencies streamline cross-border trade, it becomes clear that they offer both immediate transactional benefits and long-term strategic advantages. By embracing digital currencies, small businesses can reduce costs, eliminate exchange rate concerns, and enhance transaction security, while also positioning themselves for growth on the international stage. This journey demonstrates the transformative potential of cryptocurrencies to empower SMEs, allowing them to thrive in the global marketplace.

In the subsequent section, we will delve into specific examples of startups using cryptocurrency-based crowdfunding to fuel their growth. This shift highlights how digital currency innovation extends beyond payments to influence business funding strategies, illustrating the multifaceted impact of cryptocurrencies in creating new business opportunities.

Case Studies: Startups Thriving with Crowdfunding
Cryptocurrencies have opened new avenues for businesses engaged in cross-border trade by minimizing payment complexities and reducing fraud risks. These advantages set the stage for the emergence of cryptocurrency-based crowdfunding, allowing entrepreneurs and small businesses to explore innovative fundraising solutions. This technology-driven approach not only levels the playing field for startups across the globe but also ensures efficient and secure capital raising methods for businesses of all sizes.
Take the case of Brave, a company that ventured into the competitive realm of web browsers. Recognizing the need for privacy, they sought to change the online advertising model. Brave utilized an Initial Coin Offering (ICO) to fund their development, raising $35 million in just 30 seconds. By leveraging blockchain technology, Brave issued its native Basic Attention Token (BAT) to incentivize users. This approach provided them with a substantial capital influx, allowing the team to continue their work on enhancing user privacy and experience without traditional advertising middle-men. This demonstrated how cryptocurrency-based crowdfunding could support innovation while disrupting established business models.

Another intriguing example is Augur. This forecasting tool empowers users to make predictions on global events, combining crowdsourcing and blockchain technology. Instead of relying on traditional venture capital, Augur turned to cryptocurrency-based crowdfunding, launching its ICO and raising $5.3 million. This method of fundraising allowed Augur to harness collective insights and simultaneously build a thriving community, all while sidestepping conventional financing barriers. Their success demonstrated how strategic alignment with newer technologies facilitated better community engagement and involvement.
Steemit provides a different perspective. As a blockchain-based blogging and social

media platform, Steemit rewards users with Steem tokens for original content creation. They conducted their token sale to bootstrap the platform and incentivize participation. By distributing tokens as rewards, Steemit effectively created an ecosystem where users directly benefited from their contributions. This innovative approach not only secured the necessary funding for the platform's continued operations but also cultivated an active community of contributors and readers.

These stories highlight a recurring theme: businesses venturing beyond conventional fundraising techniques in favor of cryptocurrency-based solutions achieve not just capital, but also build vibrant communities. The success of these campaigns often relies on more than just technological innovation; it includes clear communication of value propositions and the ability to engage potential backers. Engaged communities feel an emotional investment in the project's outcomes, offering mutual benefits to both the originators and the supporters.

Looking at Basic Attention Token once more, it wasn't just the quick influx of funds that made their model compelling. It was the comprehensive feedback loop created between advertisers, publishers, and users. Users were rewarded for their attention, creating a unique advertising economy that addressed longstanding concerns about user data privacy. This strategy ensured sustained interest and growth well beyond the initial fundraising phase.

Switching gears to consider a diverse industry, the gaming sector offers a prime example of cryptocurrency-based crowdfunding through the lens of a project like MyCryptoHeroes. This blockchain-based game raised substantial funds by issuing proprietary digital assets called in-game tokens. By creating scarcity and value around these digital assets, the project attracted both gamers and investors eager to partake in a new kind of asset ownership within the gaming environment. Their method of crowdfunding effectively combined fundraising with customer acquisition, showcasing how cryptocurrency-based strategies opened up new paths for revenue generation.

Each of these examples showcases a strategic alignment with cryptocurrency's capabilities, transcending traditional fundraising boundaries. Success in this realm isn't solely dependent on the technologies used; it's about how these technologies align with the core vision of each business. Crucially, these startups capitalized on the transparency and decentralized nature of blockchain technology, which helps to alleviate potential investor concerns about fraud and misuse of funds. In doing so, they set a precedent for how businesses can foster trust and enthusiasm among both investors and customers.

Understanding these intricacies becomes pivotal as we turn our attention toward remittances and cross-border trade in the subsequent section. Both sectors stand poised to benefit from cryptocurrencies, following similar patterns of disruption and opportunity. Cryptocurrency's inherent advantages, such as reduced transaction fees and barriers to entry, mean it's not merely the domain of startups but rather a versatile tool that businesses on a global scale can exploit.

As this chapter zeroes in on the broader implications and utility of cryptocurrencies, it becomes evident how interconnected each of these innovations is. Startups, empowered by cryptocurrency-based crowdfunding, have set a precedent in fundraising, demonstrating both enhanced community participation and financial fulfillment. Meanwhile, the principles that have underscored their success will echo through discussions on how cryptocurrencies assist in remittances and cross-border trade. As businesses continue to thrive by streamlining operations and enhancing profitability, cryptocurrency stands as a keystone in reshaping financial landscapes worldwide.

Additional Case Studies: Startups Succeeding with Remittances and Cross-border Trade

Startups that successfully leveraged cryptocurrency-based crowdfunding laid the groundwork for other businesses to explore innovative financial avenues. By lowering barriers to entry, cryptocurrencies have opened up new channels for remittances and cross-border trade, offering small businesses the tools they need to thrive in a global market.

Consider a small textile company based in India. Initially, high fees and currency exchange volatility created obstacles in sourcing materials from Europe. By incorporating cryptocurrencies like Bitcoin and Ripple into their operations, the company drastically reduced transaction costs and eliminated the need for costly middlemen. This new financial freedom allowed them to reinvest in quality enhancements, leading to a 20% increase in revenue over the next year.

Cryptocurrency's role in streamlining remittance services cannot be overstated. Traditional remittance channels typically involve significant fees, slow processing times, and bureaucratic red tape, especially for small operations dealing with numerous micro-transactions. In contrast, businesses utilizing cryptocurrencies for remittance purposes experience instantaneous transfers and minimal fees, improving their bottom lines and freeing up capital for growth and innovation.

A small coffee collective in Colombia serves as another illustrative example. Their customer base in the United States often paid through traditional banking systems, which involved cumbersome procedures and delayed payments. By transitioning to cryptocurrency payments, the collective could receive funds almost immediately, significantly improving cash flow. This not only fostered customer loyalty by simplifying transactions but allowed the collective to expand their operation by quickly purchasing better equipment and hiring additional staff.

The integration of cryptocurrencies into cross-border trade extends beyond just transactional benefits. For example, a Japanese electronics startup expanded its customer reach across Asia by accepting cryptocurrencies, which facilitated seamless international sales without the need for banks to approve international transactions, which can sometimes be restrictive or delayed. This increased the startup's sales volume by 30% within six months, indicating the substantial demand and customer preference for cryptocurrency transactions.

Moreover, the transparency and security embedded within the blockchain technology that underpins most cryptocurrencies provide an additional layer of confidence in these transactions. Blockchain acts as a digital ledger, creating a verifiable chain of transaction records that users cannot alter fraudulently without consensus. This not only reassures clients and stakeholders of the integrity of transactions but also safeguards businesses against fraud and chargebacks, common issues in international trade.

Cryptocurrencies offer flexibility that caters to businesses working within fragile economies or those dealing with fluctuating national currencies. A tech firm in Argentina faced rampant inflation issues but utilized stablecoins—cryptocurrencies pegged to

stable assets like the U.S. dollar—to maintain the value of its financial resources. This strategic move protected the firm from domestic economic instability, ultimately enabling increased financial planning and investment in technology development.
Another significant consideration concerns the environmental and operational efficiency provided by cryptocurrencies in daily operations. Businesses integrating cryptocurrencies experience reduced paperwork, faster auditing processes, and enhanced customer data security, transforming their operational workflows. For example, a logistics company in Kenya reported a 50% reduction in operational costs after digitizing its payment and auditing systems through cryptocurrency. The lowered administrative burden freed up resources that could then be allocated to expanding logistics infrastructure.

This technology is also a great equalizer for women-owned businesses and those operated by other underrepresented groups. In many developing economies, women face steep financial hurdles due to a lack of access to traditional banking services. Cryptocurrencies offer these entrepreneurs a financial footprint, a safe space to save money, transact, and plan for the future of their operations without the skepticism or bias that might follow in conventional settings.
As we explore these numerous case studies, a pattern emerges that speaks to the broader potential of cryptocurrencies in reinventing how businesses operate globally. Cryptocurrencies minimize the limitations imposed by geography, politics, and traditional economic systems, enabling a new generation of entrepreneurs and small businesses to scale, innovate, and compete effectively in diverse markets.
Cryptocurrencies and their underlying technologies herald an era where businesses, irrespective of their size or history, gain equal access to state-of-the-art financial resources. It's not just about making transactions more efficient or cutting costs—though these are critical benefits. It's about crafting a resilient and adaptive business landscape where innovation propels growth, and opportunities, once limited by economic gatekeeping, become universal.

These shifts represent a profound transformation in global commerce dynamics, one that empowers those who can seize the potential of cryptocurrencies thoughtfully. With these tools at their disposal, entrepreneurs and small businesses are well-positioned to harness newfound financial agility and the security afforded by decentralized technologies.
Overall, the positive business outcomes resulting from cryptocurrency use are clear. Streamlined processes, cost savings, increased revenue, and new market access create a winsome cycle poised to enrich businesses at every stage of their growth journey. If the previous era of global trade was dominated by large multinational corporations, this burgeoning era makes space for agile startups and small enterprises, ready to spread their wings and revolutionize how we understand commerce in the global market context.

Final Insights

Cryptocurrencies are revolutionizing the way businesses navigate global markets, unlocking opportunities in crowdfunding, remittances, and cross-border trade. These digital currencies allow startups and small enterprises to overcome traditional financial barriers, enabling access to a worldwide pool of investors and customers with ease and reduced cost. By embracing cryptocurrencies, entrepreneurs can benefit from faster transactions, enhanced security, and lower fees while building vibrant communities that support their vision. As we look ahead, understanding and adopting these innovative financial tools can empower individuals and businesses, from students to policymakers, to thrive in the rapidly evolving landscape of digital finance. Now that we understand the transformative potential of cryptocurrency, we can seize new business opportunities, foster inclusive economic growth, and pave the way for sustainable development in diverse sectors across the globe.

EMPOWERING
ENTREPRENEURUS
AND SMALL BUSINESSES
SUPPORT
& RESOURCES
OPPORTUNITIES
FUNDING
GROWTH

Chapter 6: *Humanitarian Aid and Crisis Response*

Have you ever pondered how humanitarian aid reaches those in the heart of crises when chaos reigns supreme? Or wondered why, despite technological advancements, getting help to disaster-stricken areas can still be so slow and inefficient? Imagine being part of an aid organization that springs into action as soon as news of a natural disaster hits, trying your best to send life-saving supplies to affected areas. Yet, despite your urgency, logistical nightmares and bureaucratic red tape delay your efforts, leaving you scrambling to find new solutions as you watch precious time tick away.

Crises demand swift responses, yet traditional humanitarian systems often stumble on logistical hurdles, lack transparency, and face numerous barriers that hinder timely aid delivery. In this chapter, we'll delve into how innovative approaches like cryptocurrency are transforming these challenges, offering fresh pathways to make crisis response quicker, more transparent, and more efficient. Through practical examples, we'll explore how embracing these cutting-edge solutions can revolutionize the way we think about and deliver humanitarian aid during emergencies.

Introduction to Challenges in Humanitarian Aid

Humanitarian aid plays a pivotal role in crisis response by providing immediate assistance during emergencies. It is essential to rapidly deliver life-saving supplies to those affected by natural disasters, conflict, or other calamities. This aid can make the difference between life and death, as it addresses urgent needs such as food, water, shelter, and medical care, all of which are critical to alleviate suffering and support recovery efforts. However, despite its importance, delivering humanitarian aid efficiently often faces significant challenges that hamper its effectiveness.

One of the primary challenges involves logistical hurdles. In the chaos following a crisis, damaged infrastructure can impede transportation and delivery of essential goods. For instance, roads and bridges may be destroyed, making it difficult for trucks carrying supplies to reach remote or isolated communities. This was evident during the 2010 Haiti earthquake, where severe damage to ports and roads delayed the arrival and distribution of necessary aid. The challenge of overcoming such logistical obstacles requires careful planning and coordination to ensure that aid workers can reach affected areas swiftly and safely.

Another significant issue is the lack of transparency in the distribution of aid. Ensuring that aid reaches its intended recipients is crucial, yet this process is vulnerable to corruption and diversion of resources. Reports of food and supplies being sold on the black market or appropriated by local powerholders undermine the trust in aid agencies and deprive vulnerable populations of much-needed assistance. Transparency is impaired when there are inadequate systems in place to monitor and track aid flows. Improving transparency not only enhances accountability but also fosters trust between donors and recipients, ensuring that aid truly benefits those who need it most.

Delays in the deployment of resources further complicate matters. Bureaucratic procedures and administrative bottlenecks can slow down response efforts, leaving affected populations waiting longer for essential aid. In some situations, international relief agencies need to obtain permissions and clearances from governments, which can take time and hinder immediate aid delivery. The 2010 floods in Pakistan serve as an example where lengthy customs processes delayed the distribution of life-saving supplies. Quick mobilization is vital, and innovative solutions are needed to streamline these processes and reduce the bureaucratic burden, speeding up response times. Each of these challenges underscores the complexities involved in humanitarian aid delivery. Addressing logistical barriers requires investment in both infrastructure and technology that can enhance the capacity to operate in difficult conditions. Robust systems for shipping and transportation, such as airlifts or temporary bridges, alongside better-equipped local facilities and storage, can improve access to affected communities. Additionally, leveraging technology like geospatial data and real-time tracking can optimize supply routes and improve the timeliness of aid delivery.

To tackle issues of transparency, adopting digital technologies can significantly enhance the accountability of aid operations. Blockchain technology, for example, offers a way to secure transactions and provide an immutable trail of where aid is sent and received. It allows for real-time auditing and establishes trust by assuring all stakeholders that resources are utilized appropriately. Moreover, employing open platforms where donors can track donations down to granular details creates a culture of openness and accountability that can discourage corruption or mismanagement.
Reducing deployment delays requires new approaches that prioritize the swift mobilization of resources. Pre-positioning supplies in disaster-prone regions ensures that essential goods are already on-site before a crisis hits, reducing response times. Furthermore, simplifying international customs and clearance procedures through agreements and partnerships can eliminate bottlenecks that prolong the arrival of international aid. Building strong local partnerships with NGOs and government bodies is equally key to a coordinated and efficient response.

As we move towards the upcoming section, the introduction of innovative technologies like cryptocurrency offers promising solutions to some of these persistent challenges. Cryptocurrencies can expedite financial transactions, overcoming delays associated with traditional banking systems. By eliminating intermediaries and allowing for direct transfers, aid can reach local entities more efficiently, empowering them to act promptly in crises. Additionally, cryptocurrencies open new channels for crowdfunding, expanding funding sources that can be rapidly mobilized during emergencies.
In light of these challenges, adopting innovative solutions is not only necessary but urgent to transform humanitarian aid into a responsive and adaptive system. By utilizing emerging technologies and fostering collaboration across sectors, we can enhance the resilience of vulnerable communities and ensure timely and equitable delivery of aid. The shift towards incorporating cryptocurrency in disaster relief marks a significant step in overcoming the operational and logistical hurdles that have long hindered effective crisis response.

Crypto Usage in Disaster Relief

When natural disasters strike, traditional humanitarian aid systems often stumble over logistical challenges, manifesting as lengthy delays, opaque financial trails, and inefficiencies. These issues can significantly hinder the timely delivery of aid to those in dire need. The frustrations tied to these problems push us to look for alternatives, among which cryptocurrency emerges as a powerful contender. By facilitating instant financial transactions and offering greater transparency, cryptocurrency paves the way for swift support, precisely when every second counts.

Cryptocurrency changes the game by streamlining financial processes, thus increasing the speed of response dramatically. In disaster relief, the power of real-time transactions cannot be overstated. With cryptos, aid organizations can transfer funds in minutes instead of days or even weeks, a difference that can mean everything when communities are cut off from essential services or supplies. It bypasses bureaucratic red tape and directly connects relief efforts with financial resources, minimizing the intervention of middlemen that traditionally slow down the process.

Moreover, by leveraging blockchain technology, cryptocurrency ensures transparency and traceability previously unattainable with conventional systems. Every transaction recorded on a blockchain is immutable and visible to anyone with access, reassuring donors that their contributions reach the intended recipients. This builds donor confidence, which is crucial to sustaining the continuous flow of aid. Accountability increases trust, and in turn, fosters a more willing community of givers who feel certain about where and how their resources are utilized.

In practice, the adoption of cryptocurrency in disaster scenarios has already shown promise. Consider instances such as the 2015 Nepal earthquake, where cryptocurrency donations swiftly reached impacted areas despite the damaged infrastructure, enabling local organizations to mobilize faster than conventional methods allowed. This scenario serves not only as a testament to the practical application of cryptocurrency but also as an insight into its future potential. Additionally, international collaboration becomes more seamless as cryptocurrency transcends borders effortlessly, offering a unifying thread among disparate agencies, organizations, and the affected populace.

Cryptocurrency doesn't just stop at facilitating faster transactions. It also addresses another critical aspect often neglected in traditional relief - inclusivity. Local populations, sometimes unbanked or underbanked, can tap into these resources almost instantly. By employing digital wallets, which only require a smartphone, affected communities can receive aid directly, thus enabling them to prioritize and manage their needs effectively. It empowers individuals by providing them autonomy over received aid, which aligns with the principles of dignity and respect intrinsic to humanitarian efforts.

Cryptocurrency's decentralized nature opens doors to innovative funding avenues. Crowdfunding and decentralized finance (DeFi) platforms allow for collective global support, simplifying the process through which small contributions aggregate into substantial aid. Smart contracts can further transform pledges into automatic, tangible resources as soon as specific conditions are met, ensuring aid distribution promptly follows pledges. This prevents the lag between a commitment made and help delivered, again underscoring the importance of timing in life-saving missions.

For instance, in the aftermath of Hurricane Maria, Puerto Rico benefited from cryptocurrency-backed projects that funded solar kits and sustainable infrastructure solutions. These efforts showcased how linked initiatives with crypto can produce tangible results on the ground. This aspect is crucial as it illustrates crypto's role in not only immediate relief but long-term recovery and resilience building. The sustainable element is an added boon, tackling some of the root vulnerabilities exposed by disasters.

Moreover, these systems foster an environment conducive to collaboration among international entities and local agencies. Cryptocurrency's design promotes a standardized platform, ensuring all parties remain on the same page. Each party, whether it's a large international NGO or a small community-driven agency, operates from a shared ledger. This reduces duplication of efforts and brings about cohesion, which can be rare in multi-agency responses. A centralized coordination effort through decentralized technology seems paradoxical but ushers in a new era of disaster management effectiveness.

On the ground, time-sensitive interventions made possible by such instantaneous transactions can have undeniably lifesaving impacts. Picture a medical team on the front lines of a crisis, requiring urgent supplies such as insulin or blood pressure medications. If held up by cross-border banking delays, the outcomes could be catastrophic. However, with cryptocurrency, these payments proceed immediately, potentially averting tragedy. Furthermore, this efficiency propagates to other aspects of crisis management, from allocating human resources to distributing necessary equipment.

As we segue into a discussion of cryptocurrency's impact in war-torn regions, it's essential to recognize how it substantively reduces the risks associated with traditional financial operations. In volatile areas, the traditional banking system often becomes compromised either by governmental overreach or infrastructural failure. Here, the inherent security of crypto transactions offers a safer passage for funds, ensuring aid maintains its journey to those who need it, unobstructed by the tumultuous conditions. These secure, traceable transactions are less susceptible to fraud or diversion, crucial in environments where corruption might undermine conventional banking.

The potential embedded in cryptocurrency as a tool for humanitarian aid during crises is vast, breaking barriers that have long been accepted as insurmountable in disaster response. The shift from traditional methods to crypto-driven solutions could redefine our collective approach, fostering quicker responses, fostering unprecedented levels of transparency and inclusivity, and facilitating seamless international cooperation. As we explore the landscapes of war-torn areas, understanding cryptocurrency's contribution is not just an option but an imperative necessity.

Advantages of Crypto in War Zones

As we highlighted in the previous section, the role of cryptocurrency in disaster relief mainly revolves around speeding up financial transactions. This speed is crucial during emergencies when minutes can make a huge difference. Responders can get funds to the right places more quickly, avoiding delays that could risk lives. This scenario becomes even more critical in conflict zones, where traditional banking faces significant challenges like government restrictions, corrupted practices, or collapsed systems. Cryptocurrencies eliminate the red tape and vulnerabilities that come with traditional systems. They help workers respond swiftly by transmitting funds to recipients directly, without needing intermediaries who might slow things down or mishandle resources. Think of them as a streamlined solution where each transaction is swift and secure, making a complex task simpler. This kind of efficiency is not just about faster help; it's about ensuring aid reaches the actual people in need, not lost somewhere within the flaws of outdated systems.

Take Syria, for example, where financial infrastructures were badly affected by war. Traditional banking couldn't be applied with ease. Here, cryptocurrencies came to the rescue. People turned to platforms that enabled Bitcoin transactions, facilitating transfers that cut through potential hindrances that beset conventional systems. Such transactions don't require a fixed address or rely on local banking facilities, providing a crucial breakthrough. Even humanitarian organizations utilized cryptocurrencies to deliver much-needed assistance without dealing with problematic local banking systems. With cryptocurrencies, funds arrived safely and quickly with lower transaction costs, benefiting the end-users directly impacted by conflict.

In Venezuela, amid a severe economic breakdown exacerbated by hyperinflation, people and organizations adopted cryptocurrencies as a lifeline. International aid groups found cryptocurrencies especially useful here, bypassing inefficient banking systems crippled by hyperinflation and government interference. The move away from relying completely on their local currency to using stable coins and Bitcoin made funds accessible and valuable, irrespective of local economic conditions.

The success in these situations isn't just about technology; it's about how technology aligns with local needs and constraints. Cryptocurrencies offer versatility, anonymity, and a new avenue amid chaotic environments. They help to distribute aid with minimal friction and maximum security, bypassing barriers that would typically cut off access to crucial resources. They're essentially redefining how aid reaches its destination and ensuring fewer individuals fall through the cracks of bureaucratic hurdles.

Understanding the technical side, blockchain technology backs cryptocurrencies. It operates on different properties like decentralization and transparency which can essentially counterbalance challenges presented by conflict settings. These attributes prove vital in war zones where fear of fraud, theft, or currency devaluation can pose serious threats. Each transaction is verified multiple times, ensuring funds are tracked, yet still secure from tampering.

Moreover, because cryptocurrencies don't rely on banking hours or locations, they fit into the unpredictable rhythm of crisis scenarios. When access to banks may be unreliable or even impossible, aid workers find cryptocurrencies a consistent and trustworthy asset that continues to operate non-stop, delivering what's required whenever and wherever needed.

Yet, it's not all perfect. Challenges remain like the need for tech literacy among both receivers and aid providers. Technical infrastructure is necessary, too, to facilitate these transactions. Even with an immediate need for speed and tight data security, stakeholders must ensure that they build and secure systems robustly to provide essentials like electricity and internet access in regions where these are not guaranteed. This facet still requires focused efforts to optimize where solutions can serve best regardless of local limitations.

Furthermore, regulatory issues and local acceptance of cryptocurrencies pose hurdles which still need attention. Legal frameworks and understanding around cryptocurrencies yet need clarity in many regions. Governments must establish supportive policies and educational programs to help integrate these solutions more fully.

Despite these challenges, it's clear the potential far outweighs the negatives in emergencies. Utilizing cryptocurrencies has proven critical when peeling bureaucratic layers that slow down the aid process. These swift, efficient vehicles of aid are not only about immediate life support but also pave the path for rebuilding and relief in more sustainable ways. Even amidst war's unpredictability, the ability of cryptocurrencies to dodge conventional hurdles and offering clear, efficient pathways leaves a lasting mark

on humanitarian efforts' future.
Looking forward, as humanitarian organizations consider the many upsides of cryptocurrencies, they aim to streamline processes where bureaucracy slows action. Although hurdles remain, especially with access and education, the success stories reinforce the importance of revolutionizing how aid gets delivered. What's emerging is a period where digital currencies don't just represent a secondary option but stand as a preferred solution to ongoing challenges in humanitarian aid distribution. This transformation signifies more than a technological shift; it opens doors to innovative strategies where technological resilience mirrors human resilience, reinforcing the future of aid in crisis resolution.

As we move to the next section, let's think about how these transformative mechanisms help sidestep the cumbersome bureaucracies that commonly bog down aid delivery. Consider how cultivating efficiency can dismantle roadblocks in management and procedural norms, shedding light on the dynamic role cryptocurrencies play in making sure help reaches those clamoring for relief without unnecessary delay.

Bypassing Bureaucracy for Direct Aid Delivery
Cryptocurrency has emerged as a pivotal player in the realm of humanitarian aid by reducing risks associated with traditional banking systems, especially in regions plagued by war. Unlike conventional methods that often require heavy reliance on banking institutions, cryptocurrency offers a direct pathway for transferring funds, thus minimizing exposure to potential threats like fund misappropriation or bureaucratic delays. Bypassing traditional banking systems enables the flow of resources to occur with increased speed and security. These advantages lay the groundwork for our exploration into strategic measures crafted to slice through bureaucratic red tape in the delivery of aid.
Strategies that dismantle bureaucratic obstacles in aid delivery are essential in humanitarian contexts. These approaches are like master keys, unlocking the channels through which crucial resources can reach those in distress. For instance, smart contracts, which are self-executing agreements with the terms directly written into lines of code, play a critical role here. They automate transactions and reduce the need for intermediaries. By doing so, these contracts ensure that funds are deployed exactly where they're needed without the usual administrative overhead. Smart contracts can trigger immediate release of funds when predefined conditions are met, streamlining the process and ensuring transparency.

Decentralized finance, or DeFi, is another avenue being pursued for cutting through bureaucratic layers. DeFi platforms operate on blockchain technology, offering financial transactions without the need for centralized financial intermediaries. These platforms allow for the creation of financial tools that work independently of traditional banking systems. In humanitarian efforts, DeFi can facilitate peer-to-peer transactions, enabling donors to provide aid directly to beneficiaries. The absence of central authorities in DeFi systems means that transactions are both efficient and less prone to corrupt practices, ensuring that resources are allocated correctly and swiftly.
Blockchain technology's capacity for providing transparent records can also circumvent bureaucratic complications. Each transaction recorded on a blockchain is immutable and visible to all parties involved. This transparency ensures accountability and minimizes opportunities for corruption. For organizations distributing aid, this visibility

means they can track donations in real time and confirm that supplies or funds reach their intended destinations. In situations where oversight is critical, blockchain technology offers an unprecedented level of trust in the systems used to manage aid. The use of mobile wallets is surging as another effective tool in overcoming bureaucratic barriers. These digital wallets are particularly advantageous in areas where access to traditional banking is limited. With mobile phones being widely available, especially in developing regions, recipients of aid can receive cryptocurrency directly to their mobile wallets. This method ensures that even those in remote or conflict-torn regions can access financial support with minimal delay. Mobile wallets eliminate the need for physical bank branches, reducing the layers through which aid must traditionally pass.

One compelling example of these strategies at work is found in the response to the Syrian refugee crisis. Traditional aid routes often slowed the distribution of resources, leading to delays in essential supplies reaching refugee camps. By employing cryptocurrency, aid organizations were able to circumvent these slow-moving processes. In one initiative, emergency coins were distributed to refugees via blockchain, allowing them to purchase food and supplies directly from local vendors, thus bolstering the local economy while also addressing immediate needs. These emergency coins function as both a life-saving tool and a testament to how innovation in aid distribution can occur when conventional routes prove obstructive.
Consider the efforts in Venezuela, where hyperinflation has rendered the national currency almost valueless. Aid organizations have turned to cryptocurrency to provide effective support. Using digital currencies, these organizations deliver aid directly to Venezuelans in dire need, bypassing the faltering local economy and government controls. By doing so, they ensure that families can access necessities like food and medicine without the risk of devaluation. The success of these initiatives highlights the profound impact of employing cryptocurrency in circumventing economic and political hindrances that traditional methods cannot navigate.

As we move toward the next section on direct aid initiatives using crypto, it's important to recognize that what we've explored so far is merely the foundation for a deeper dive into specific instances of crypto's transformative influence. We will analyze case studies where these innovative strategies have tangibly improved the efficiency and effectiveness of humanitarian operations. The upcoming discussion will further cement your understanding of the utility of cryptocurrency in aid delivery, allowing us to build on what we've discussed and witnessed.
In breaking through bureaucratic barriers, innovative solutions enable aid to act swiftly and securely. Each strategy discussed here, from smart contracts and blockchain transparency to mobile wallets, encapsulates how technology is repurposing and enhancing humanitarian efforts. The seamless transition back to examples of direct applications ensures that this exploration remains grounded in real-world practice, providing clarity and insight as we move forward in unraveling the comprehensive application of crypto in humanitarian contexts.

Case Studies of Successful Direct Aid Delivery

In the previous section, we examined strategies to navigate bureaucratic obstacles, aiming to streamline the process of aid delivery. Now, let's explore how the use of cryptocurrency has advanced these efforts. Direct aid initiatives using cryptocurrency have shown remarkable promise in improving the speed and efficiency of humanitarian aid. In situations where conventional systems falter, often tied up in red tape and sluggish approval processes, crypto-based solutions step in as nimble alternatives for distributing aid. The speed at which cryptocurrency can be transferred sidesteps many delays inherent in traditional methods. Through the lens of real-world examples, we can appreciate just how profound this transformation can be.

Consider the case of the United Nations World Food Program (WFP) deploying a blockchain-based payment system named Building Blocks. This platform was piloted in Jordan's Azraq camp, home to thousands of Syrian refugees. Building Blocks allowed aid to be transferred directly to beneficiaries in the form of crypto-tokens that could be redeemed at local supermarkets equipped with biometric scanners. This system bypassed the need for cash or intermediary banking services, ensuring that each transaction was transparent and recorded securely on the blockchain. Consequently, this approach reduced overhead costs, sped up the distribution of aid, and enhanced security, a key concern in humanitarian crises.

Similarly, in Venezuela, a country grappling with economic instability and hyperinflation, the program "Save the Children" used Bitcoin as a medium to fund crucial supplies and resources for Venezuelan residents. By utilizing cryptocurrency, they were able to bypass the failing local banking systems, and ensure aid reached those who needed it swiftly and securely, even amidst significant financial turmoil. This not only demonstrated the adaptability of cryptocurrencies in various environments but also provided a blueprint for similar initiatives in other regions facing economic crises.

However, the adoption of crypto-based aid isn't without its challenges. One significant hurdle is the volatility of cryptocurrencies. The value of digital currencies can fluctuate wildly, which can complicate budgeting and aid predictability. Another issue is the general lack of infrastructure and knowledge about cryptocurrencies in many areas where humanitarian aid is most needed. Many communities do not possess access to the internet or mobile technology necessary to utilize or understand these novel systems. This highlights a digital divide that, if not addressed, creates barriers to the benefits that cryptocurrency-based aid systems offer.

Moreover, regulatory uncertainties in various countries pose another challenge. In some regions, governments do not yet have clear policies regarding the use of cryptocurrencies, which can lead to legal complications or restrictions on crypto-based activities. The lack of regulation can also contribute to concerns about security and fraud, potentially putting vulnerable populations at risk.

Nevertheless, these challenges also present opportunities for growth and innovation in the use of cryptocurrencies for humanitarian aid. Lessons from these challenges drive home the importance of developing stablecoins—cryptocurrencies designed to have a stable value tied to a reserve asset—to mitigate volatility risks. For instance, using stablecoins such as Tether (USDT) or USD Coin (USDC) for aid transfers can offer a more reliable digital cash experience, ensuring recipients receive a consistent value.

In addressing the digital divide, partnerships with mobile providers to increase connectivity in underserved areas has been pivotal. Additionally, training programs aimed at enhancing digital literacy can empower communities to fully harness the potential of digital aid platforms. For example, in Kenya, initiatives are underway to provide educational workshops that teach locals not just about cryptocurrency, but also about broader digital financial systems, granting them greater control over their personal finances and building long-term self-sufficiency.

Policymakers also have a role to play in shaping an environment that both welcomes innovation and safeguards communities. Establishing frameworks that clarify the legal use of cryptocurrencies can foster trust and encourage adoption while protecting populations from potential misuse. Regulators, however, must strike a balance between enabling innovation and ensuring that safeguards are in place to protect against fraud and abuse.

Looking ahead, the transformative potential of cryptocurrency to reshape humanitarian aid is immense. It paves the way for more direct and expedited aid processes, cutting through delays and bottlenecks that have long hampered timely responses to crises. Moreover, as digital and financial literacy improves, more communities will be able to engage with these systems seamlessly. It's about cultivating an ecosystem where everyone can participate and benefit.

Ultimately, the successful deployment and reception of cryptocurrency in humanitarian aid underscore its power as a tool for positive change. While the journey comes with challenges, the insights gained along the way highlight pathways to enhanced impact and efficacy. Each incremental improvement in digital accessibility, regulatory clarity, and technological integration brings us closer to a system where help arrives not just in time, but also in a form that empowers its recipients. As we continue exploring these avenues, the ideal of efficient, direct, and transformative humanitarian aid supported by cryptocurrencies becomes not just a possibility but a growing reality.

Final Insights

As we've explored, innovative solutions like cryptocurrency are reshaping the landscape of humanitarian aid by surmounting logistical challenges and improving transparency and efficiency. Cryptocurrencies enable direct, rapid financial transactions in crisis zones, bypassing red tape and avoiding traditional banking woes, whether amidst natural disasters or war-torn regions. By leveraging technology such as blockchain, we ensure that aid reaches those who need it most with increased accountability and reduced corruption risks. Looking forward, the potential of these technologies to revolutionize aid delivery is immense. As more regions gain digital access and financial literacy improves, the adoption of crypto-based systems will likely grow, fostering quicker responses and empowering communities worldwide. Armed with these insights, we can push toward a future where aid is timely, effective, and equitable, truly embodying the spirit of innovation in humanitarian efforts.

Chapter 7: *Wealth Creation and New Opportunities*

Wealth Creation and New Opportunities

In a bustling café in the heart of the city, Sarah sat with a steaming cup of coffee in hand, scrolling through her phone. The latest headlines flashed across her screen: "Cryptocurrency Hits Record Highs" and "Blockchain Revolutionizes Finance." Sarah, like many others, felt a mix of intrigue and bewilderment. The world of digital finance seemed tantalizingly close, yet frustratingly complex. She remembered the stories she'd heard about friends of friends who had struck gold with early investments in cryptocurrencies and blockchain projects. These tales were compelling, painting an image of endless opportunities just waiting to be seized. But for Sarah, as someone new to this universe, every step felt steeped in technical jargon, and uncertainty clouded her enthusiasm.

Sarah's experience mirrors that of countless individuals navigating the landscape of modern finance, where the promise of wealth creation dances alongside the specter of risk. As digital currencies reshape the financial terrain, people are drawn by the potential for growth but are also wary of the traps hidden beneath the surface. In this chapter, we delve into these new pathways for financial advancement, emphasizing the importance of early adoption and cautious participation. By shedding light on the tools and insights needed to navigate this evolving space, we aim to empower you to make informed decisions, unlocking new opportunities for wealth creation.

Introduction to Wealth Creation and New Opportunities

Many of us are looking for ways to build wealth in today's fast-paced world, and a key place to start is understanding how digital finance is reshaping the landscape. While the basic concept of wealth creation isn't new, the tools at our disposal certainly are. Recent technological advances offer new paths to financial growth, opening doors to opportunities that simply didn't exist before.

The idea of digital finance encompasses a wide range of innovations. From cryptocurrencies to blockchain technology, these new methods of handling and transferring money are rapidly gaining ground. As these technologies develop, they present unique chances for individuals and businesses to grow their wealth. The key is to recognize these opportunities early on, positioning oneself to take full advantage of what these tools can offer.

Early adoption is particularly important in a field that moves as quickly as digital finance. Digital currencies have shown significant growth potential in the past decade, and those who were quick to recognize their value have benefitted greatly. Yet, this rapid pace also brings challenges, primarily the risk of engaging with systems that aren't fully understood. Therefore, a cautious approach—one that balances enthusiasm with due diligence—is critical for anyone looking to explore these financial pathways.

Why should this matter to you? Because the potential for wealth creation through digital finance is significant. For example, take Bitcoin, one of the most well-known cryptocurrencies. While many were initially skeptical, Bitcoin's value and prominence have grown, proving that there's merit in taking calculated risks. Investors who entered the Bitcoin market early have seen exponential growth in their investments, something

that highlights the advantage of being a first mover.
But cryptocurrencies are just one piece of the puzzle. Innovative financial mechanisms like peer-to-peer lending and decentralized finance platforms are rapidly changing how people engage with money. Peer-to-peer lending allows individuals to lend money directly to others, bypassing traditional financial institutions. This can provide investors with higher returns, as they earn interest on their loans, while also offering borrowers lower interest rates than those typically charged by banks.

Similarly, decentralized finance, or DeFi, is democratizing access to different financial products. These platforms operate without traditional banks, meaning transactions can happen at any time and are accessible to anyone with an internet connection. It's a transformative approach to finance that could dramatically alter how we interact with money. With DeFi, one can engage in activities like trading, lending, and borrowing in a decentralized manner, benefiting from lower fees and easier access.
To make these concepts easier to understand, consider a simple example. Imagine you're able to lend your money directly to someone halfway across the world without dealing with a bank or other intermediaries. You're in control of your investment decisions, and the borrower benefits from lower interest costs. This is the kind of connection digital finance facilitates and transpires in systems like DeFi.
Navigating these opportunities requires a blend of technical understanding and strategic insight. Thankfully, the digital finance community is full of resources ranging from online courses to forums where beginners can educate themselves. By building a strong foundation of knowledge, newcomers can better position themselves to take advantage of the emerging opportunities.

Let's not overlook the role of technology in making this more accessible. Today, there are numerous apps and platforms that help simplify digital finance. They offer user-friendly interfaces that demystify complex financial activities, making them more approachable for everyday users. These tools often provide tutorials and guides, helping you learn as you go. So, whether you're investing in cryptocurrency or exploring peer-to-peer lending, you have support at your fingertips.
However, as with any investment, there are risks involved. Digital finance is subject to market volatility, and the lack of regulation can add an extra layer of risk. It's crucial to stay informed about the market conditions and potential legal changes that might affect your investments. Diversification—spreading your money across different types of investments—can help mitigate some risks, balancing higher-risk opportunities with more stable options.
The appeal of digital finance isn't just the possibility of earning money. Many are drawn to the idea of being part of a movement that is disrupting traditional industries and making finance more inclusive. The decentralized nature of these financial systems means that individuals can regain control over their financial lives, no longer reliant on the whims of big institutions.

Understanding these changes helps prepare individuals to take advantage of the opportunities they present. The combination of early adoption, proactive learning, and strategic application sets the stage for significant financial breakthroughs. As we transition to the next topic, consider how embracing these changes can lead to not only personal financial growth but can also contribute to shaping the future of finance. By staying informed and actively participating in the waves of innovation, you position yourself to make the most of these wealth-building opportunities in digital finance.

The Role of Early Adopters in Investment Success

Having wrapped up our overview of emerging opportunities in wealth creation, let's segue into the fascinating role of early adopters. Early adoption is a critical factor for those aiming to ride the financial success wave. By being at the forefront of emerging market trends, individuals gain firsthand opportunities to tap into the potential that others may overlook. This is not merely about being the first to act but rather being the first to understand and align with changing dynamics, creating an impactful strategy for wealth accumulation.

Consider the curious case of Bitcoin, where individuals who dabbled in cryptocurrencies at their inception found themselves in unexpectedly advantageous positions. One such example is Erik Finman, a teenager at the time, who invested $1,000 in Bitcoin when they were priced at just $12 per coin. Fast forward, and the value of those coins surged exponentially, showcasing a profound financial breakthrough courtesy of early adoption. These early adopters did not just buy a digital asset; they purchased a ticket to the evolving narrative of financial technology, one that has written significant wealth stories.

It's crucial to delve into why early adoption ushers in such transformative financial potential. Early entry typically comes with lower costs and the possibility for higher returns. This initial risk is mitigated by the often-staggering growth associated with nascent technology or marketable concepts. Simply put, the earlier you venture in, the more extended runway you have for potential gains. However, understanding the lingo and mechanisms is essential. Cryptocurrencies, for instance, come with terminologies like blockchain, decentralization, and tokens, which might sound cryptic at first. In reality, a blockchain is simply a digital ledger that records transactions across many computers. Understanding these terms simplifies the entire investment process.

The balance of risks and rewards also plays a pivotal role here. While early adoption presents golden opportunities, it doesn't come without its share of uncertainties. Recall the early days of the internet; investors took massive leaps of faith on concepts that appeared abstract at the time. Yet, those who participated witnessed booming success, as commonplace companies today were once just mysterious names with futuristic promises.

The transformative power of early adoption isn't restricted to cryptocurrencies or tech startups. Other sectors like renewable energy, biotech, and artificial intelligence show similar potential. For instance, early investments in companies developing disruptive solar technologies or those working on groundbreaking pharmaceutical solutions have historically yielded stellar returns. The common thread here is recognizing potential before it becomes mainstream and taking calculated leaps of faith.

Now, why do some individuals seize these opportunities while others watch from the sidelines? It often boils down to a blend of curiosity, education, and strategic risk management. Early adopters tend to keep a finger on the pulse of innovation, constantly learning and adapting. Access to information, networking in relevant circles, and staying attuned to market shifts are critical habits. Moreover, they adopt a balance between optimistic foresight and prudent skepticism, carefully weighing potential downsides against the prospect of rewards.

To further build trust with the reader, let's dive into a practical example: think about an educator who perceives the growth potential of online education platforms driven by AI.

Rather than feeling overwhelmed, they leverage their understanding of AI—from algorithms to personalized learning experiences—to invest early in companies developing such technologies. Over time, as digital education becomes integral, the investment's value appreciates significantly, underscoring how early adoption and industry knowledge culminate in financial success.

It's essential to note that this conversation isn't just for the individual investor seeking to convert a modest sum into fortune. Policy makers and educators too stand at the pivotal point of adopting innovative frameworks and fostering environments where these opportunities are widely accessible. By understanding and capitalizing on early adoption's benefits, they can craft policies and curricula that resonate with contemporary financial landscapes, making emerging opportunities tangible for broader communities.

As we ease toward the next section, we're setting the stage to examine how early adoption not only drives investment success but also leads to life-altering outcomes. We'll explore actual instances where individuals' foresight and initiative have turned dreams into reality, embodying the profound effect of stepping into opportunities when others hesitate. Through these narratives, we aim to inspire and illustrate that wealth creation isn't merely about accruing assets. It's about making informed decisions, embracing progress, and changing one's story in potentially transformative ways. Let us prepare to explore how these outcomes unfold and redefine what wealth means in our changing world, continuing this journey through the landscape of new financial possibilities together.

Key Life-Changing Investments and Their Impacts

In the previous section, we discussed how some individuals leveraged early adoption to achieve financial growth. These pioneers in the world of digital assets found themselves navigating uncharted territories. Despite skepticism, their ventures brought unmatched success, proving that seizing the moment can alter the course of one's life.

A vivid example of this dynamic is the story of a young software developer, who saw Bitcoin's potential in its infancy. Back in 2010, when Bitcoin was priced at mere cents, he started mining using a modest computer setup. While others couldn't see beyond Bitcoin's abstract nature, he recognized its promise as a decentralized currency. His initial investment of time and technical interest, rather than substantial capital, laid the groundwork for a future windfall. By 2017, with Bitcoin exceeding $10,000, his portfolio was valued in the millions. The success of this developer underscores the significance of discerning trends early and capitalizing on them.

This developer's journey wasn't just luck; it was a mix of technical knowledge, curiosity, and fortuity. His approach wasn't only about buying low and selling high. Instead, he deeply engaged with the technology, contributing to online forums, sharing insights, and participating in the broader conversation shaping Bitcoin's trajectory. By doing so, he gained invaluable, firsthand knowledge of both the short-term fluctuations and the long-term potential of cryptocurrency.

Similarly, consider the story of a group of friends from New York who pooled their resources to invest in Ethereum's initial coin offering (ICO) in 2014. At the time, Ethereum was a nascent concept, emphasizing smart contracts and decentralized applications. Despite its innovative promise, it remained an enigma to mainstream investors. These friends, however, understood the blockchain's potential beyond cryptocurrency. Each chipped in a few thousand dollars, motivated by a shared vision of a decentralized future. With Ethereum's exponential rise, their collective investment turned into a staggering eight-figure sum, transforming their financial prospects overnight.

What stands out in these narratives isn't just their outcomes but the strategic decisions they undertook. Both cases involved recognizing technological innovations and understanding their implications. This level of insight required constant learning, vigilance, and often, going against the grain of conventional financial wisdom. It also meant having a certain risk tolerance—a willingness to face potential losses for the chance of substantial gains.

Investors exhibit different styles. Some, like our developer friend, dive deep into the technicalities, while others, like the New York group, rely on collaborative efforts and communal wisdom to inform their investment strategies. Regardless of the method, a common thread ties these success stories: foresight.

Now, let's delve into the mechanics. Firstly, timing was a crucial factor. Each of these early adopters joined the crypto world during its nascent stages, when mainstream understanding was limited. This allowed them to purchase assets at significantly lower prices. Secondly, there was a commitment to learning and adapting. Crypto isn't static; it evolves. Early investors not only acquired assets but also absorbed new information, staying ahead of emerging trends.

Furthermore, strategic diversification within the crypto sphere played a role. Those who diversified their holdings often buffered against losses in the volatile market. They spread investments across various promising projects, mitigating risks while allowing room to benefit from multiple success stories.

In the case of the Ethereum investors, their foresight extended to understanding the broader implications of blockchain technology. They didn't view Ethereum solely as a cryptocurrency but as a platform for change, with smart contracts that could disrupt industries. This wider perspective allowed them to appreciate Ethereum's potential beyond immediate financial gains.

It's important to emphasize strategic patience. While these investors were part of an early wave, they weren't day traders. Instead, they held onto their investments, weathering cycles of price volatility. Their patience paid off as their assets matured at a time when the world began acknowledging the value of digital currencies.

The life-altering outcomes these early adopters experienced serve as compelling reminders of the opportunities embedded in being first movers. These stories demonstrate that by adopting a forward-thinking mindset and an openness to new technologies, individuals can position themselves at the forefront of financial breakthroughs.

Yet, these tales of triumph are not solely meant to inspire wild optimism. They should also prepare us for the subsequent discussion on the potential risks involved in digital investments. While rewards can be immense, the possibility of substantial losses exists. Understanding the delicate balance between risks and rewards becomes essential for those wishing to navigate the crypto landscape responsibly.

As we move into the next section, we'll explore these risks in detail, underscoring the importance of informed, careful participation in the digital investment world. The narrative will guide you through evaluating these risks while considering the immense potential rewards. Ensuring our decisions are balanced and informed can help us not only capitalize on opportunities but also safeguard our financial well-being. Recognizing the transformative potential of early adoption is crucial, yet embracing it with eyes wide open is equally important. Through smart investments informed by thorough research and a keen understanding of market dynamics, we can unlock opportunities that technology presents—responsibly and with foresight.

Understanding Risks and Rewards in Wealth Creation

From life-changing investments to understanding new opportunities, early adopters reveal a mixed bag of successes and lessons learned. Their experiences aren't just lucky breaks; they form a roadmap through which new entrants can evaluate the potential of financial opportunities. As we stand on this foundation, we embrace a core challenge—understanding the balance between risk and reward that lies ahead. Stepping into new financial waters like cryptocurrencies and blockchain technologies necessitates more than just enthusiasm. It's about acknowledging the landscape dotted with towering promises and lurking pitfalls. The appeal of these technologies isn't hard to see. With their promise of decentralization and freedom from traditional financial institutions, blockchain and cryptocurrencies command attention. Yet, this potential carries intrinsic volatility, a factor our exploratory path cannot ignore.

Take, for instance, the whirlwind journey of Bitcoin. Its rise sparked excitement as values soared to astronomical heights. Early adopters, who bought in when prices were low, capitalized on this surge. Their returns became the stuff of legend, drawing headlines and setting off a rush comparable to a modern gold rush. However, just as fortunes could be made, they could just as quickly exact heavy losses. Markets saw downturns, leaving some investors grappling with financial uncertainty. Despite its technological appeal, Bitcoin remains a volatile market, with values susceptible to external factors ranging from regulatory news to investor sentiment.

Ethereum, another heavyweight in the crypto space, offers lessons in both growth and caution. Lauded for its smart contract capabilities, Ethereum enabled a swath of new enterprises. Startups flocked to its platform, offering innovations that pushed the boundaries of what blockchain technology could accomplish. Yet, as Ethereum's technological promise took center stage, issues of scalability and network congestion emerged. Users experienced slower transaction times and higher costs, a reminder that technological innovation doesn't travel a problem-free path. Investors and businesses, drawn to its potential, needed awareness and adaptability when mitigating the risks involved.

In the crypto realm, the initial coin offering (ICO) frenzy unveiled yet another layer of complexity. ICOs democratized access to fundraising, granting startups an unprecedented way to gather capital. For investors, these offerings promised entry into innovative ventures. ICOs greeted with optimism, embodied both opportunity and risk. The downside? A lack of regulation fostered rampant fraudulent schemes, causing investors to lose billions. Yet, ICOs also funded legitimate businesses that evolved into industry leaders. This dichotomy speaks to the essence of understanding risk—it's not just about chasing the next big thing; it's about discerning genuine prospects from risky ventures.

Consider the rise of non-fungible tokens (NFTs). Revolutionary in its approach, NFTs offer digital ownership through blockchain. Art, music, and collectibles experienced a digital renaissance, allowing creators direct interaction with audiences. For investors, NFTs became a new frontier for value appreciation. Much like earlier crypto adventures, NFTs showcased both astounding profits and sudden crashes. The story of digital artist Beeple's NFT art auctioned for millions demonstrated the eye-popping potential of the market. Yet, like any market, the value of art remains subjective, prone to shifts in demand and hype cycles. Investors guided by nothing but social media buzz risked encountering losses. The key takeaway? As investor interest heightens, a balanced evaluation of both the potential and hype is essential.

Assessing these stories alongside others, it's clear that the lure of financial growth colors our perception of the risks. Yet, recognizing that risk is ever-present, not inherently bad, frames decision-making processes. It teaches that while reward tempts our senses, caution becomes our ally. Real-life testimonials transform theoretical risk into relatable narratives. The stories of those who've succeeded or faced setbacks illuminate the path for others. Their shared insights color the tapestry of cautionary yet promising tales. These accounts underscore the need to approach investments in the crypto world—not with blind optimism, but with an evaluative mindset.

But what steps can readers take for responsible engagement? Firstly, education is paramount. The more informed you become, the more equipped you are in navigating potential pitfalls. Delve into understanding each investment—what are its underlying principles, its market drivers, and its potential obstacles? Engage with communities and trusted sources offering balanced perspectives. This foundational knowledge helps demystify complexities and guides decisions with the lens of reality.

Next, diversification remains a safeguard tool. Just as you wouldn't place all your eggs in one basket, diversifying investments mitigates risk exposure. It's about building layered financial strategies, allowing one part of your portfolio the room to soar while another guards stable growth. The act of balancing fosters resilience within financial landscapes.

Furthermore, understanding our behavior becomes a hidden strength. Human nature often inclines towards impulse decisions, especially in volatile markets. Recognizing this bias encourages a pause—a critical break for reassessment and rationality. Align decisions with long-term goals rather than transient market reactions.

Drawing these threads together, we recognize that opportunities provide more than a path to wealth; they offer a mirrored reflection of the choices we make. It's about the convergence of knowledge, caution, and strategic foresight. Our journey here emphasizes not just the potential of financial adoption but the responsibility accompanying it. As you navigate further, the discussion will naturally evolve. We'll take the insights from this section to underscore the role of informed decision-making in sustaining market growth and stability. One step at a time, armed with understanding and caution, you build a more resilient financial future.

Importance of Responsible Participation in Financial Growth

In the last section, the focus was on the potential risks and rewards of financial opportunities. This is the perfect segue into how responsible engagement and decision-making can transform these opportunities into real financial growth. Now, we hone our lens on the ways to safely and intelligently navigate these new financial terrains. The allure of financial markets today is undeniable, especially with emerging digital assets. But with every allure comes the necessity for caution and decisiveness.

Imagine you're standing at the crossroads of innovation, digital assets promising to change the way the world handles finances. Early adopters stand to gain tremendously if they navigate with care. Think about those who embraced e-commerce at its dawn—they laid down frameworks which not only rewarded them but also helped shape the current vast digital marketplace. They didn't leap blindly; their success came from informed decisions and measured risks.

Consider a startup company that pivoted early to accept cryptocurrency payments. In 2017, they were part of a niche group, innovators at the forefront of a new wave. Fast forward to 2020, and they'd not only increased their market reach but had also grown their financial portfolio significantly. The secret? They had a well-thought-out strategy that included educating their workforce and understanding the shifting regulatory landscape.

These examples can seem distant for an individual starting on their journey on financial growth. Let's personalize this. You're contemplating whether to include digital assets in your investment portfolio. The first smart move is research. Educate yourself about the digital marketplace. Look beyond internet headlines to understand crypto's Blockchain foundation. Grasp how these technologies can integrate with existing financial systems—because understanding opens doors to inspiration and innovation.

Another method to engage responsibly is diversifying your portfolio. When venturing into new financial opportunities, it's crucial to have a right mix of traditional and digital assets. You mitigate risks by not putting all your eggs in one basket. Just like Dan, a young investor who diversified his 401(k) by allocating a modest percentage to crypto, felt apprehensive at first. He kept a steady pace, informed by consistent updates from reliable financial advisors and platforms. As the newest keywords in financial stability and growth evolve, this balance between conservative and innovative plays made Dan's venture a successful learning curve.

Conversations around wealth creation and digital assets always intersect with technology. These innovations are enabling newer, faster transactions, and widening access. For instance, micro-investments through apps allow users to invest with spare change. What was once an overwhelming concept is now available to teenagers fresh out of high school. Partnerships between tech companies and financial institutions are crafting pathways to inclusivity, allowing communities previously barred by technical complexity to participate in wealth generation.

Regulation and education walk hand in hand in the financial world. Markets are no longer the Wild West of the past, but this doesn't mean that due diligence disappears. Many nations are crafting policies to harness digital markets' potential within secure frameworks. As an investor or business, keep abreast of these regulatory shifts. These checks and balances ensure markets don't spiral into unsafe waters. They guard against volatility, offering an added layer of safety. This is as essential as understanding the financial product itself.

The journey to financial literacy is lifelong, and knowledge is invaluable in making informed decisions. A practical step forward involves joining networks, attending workshops, and staying connected with market trends. Harness social media and professional platforms to follow thought leaders in finance and technology. This doesn't just keep you informed but also offers a sense of community, shared interests, and collective intelligence guiding your decisions.

For businesses, the conversation shifts slightly to integrating digital assets into existing portfolios. It begins with internal audits of your financial strategies—does digital alignment enhance your objectives? Developing internal capabilities to support such transitions isn't just trendy, it's smart. Wave, a small business accounting software company, rolled out options to integrate Bitcoin payments. Their client base inched higher not only because the payment methods expanded, but their transparent communication around these changes reassured traditional clients. This is a classic case of innovation syncing with client trust.

For established financial institutions, engaging with startups and fintech companies creates hybrid ecosystems. Collaborations offer insights into agile frameworks, allowing larger entities to pivot into digital spaces more smoothly. These partnerships bring out the best of both worlds—the nimbleness of new intel with the experience of established capital rules.

Every successful engagement in the financial markets traces back to considered, informed decision-making. It surfaces in the stories of individuals and organizations who took the leap with eyes wide open, cognizant of both the promise and perils of digital assets. It's about being adaptable and staying grounded. Such an approach reduces exposure to losses and attracts growth.

Navigating the evolving landscape of financial opportunities isn't about speed, but about having a calculated approach. Listening and learning remain key to unlocking new doors. This section underlines that wealth isn't just an accumulation of assets, but also knowledge, strategies, and networks. It isn't enough to adopt early—you must create a sustainable practice of learning and executing well-thought-out plans.

Wherever your journey in wealth creation takes you, fundamental tenets like education, diversification, community engagement, regulation consideration, and strategic collaboration are invaluable. It's the confluence of these strategies that equips you to ride the wave of financial opportunity responsibly.

Final Insights

As we wrap up this chapter on financial growth through early adoption and careful participation, the message is clear: by understanding new technologies like digital finance, individuals can harness vast opportunities for wealth creation. Early movers have historically reaped enormous benefits, yet it's essential to couple enthusiasm with cautious due diligence. Now that we've delved into the landscape of cryptocurrencies, peer-to-peer lending, and decentralized finance systems, we have a solid foundation to explore these digital avenues confidently. Embracing fast-paced changes while remaining informed and prudent will not only help you navigate potential pitfalls but also align you to thrive in the evolving financial ecosystem. Whether you're a newcomer, investor, professional, or policymaker, informed decisions and strategic participation lead to financial empowerment. By staying curious, seeking educational resources, and collaborating within thriving communities, you are well-positioned to contribute to shaping the future of finance responsibly.

WEALTH CREATION
AND NEW OPPORTUNITIES
ECONOMIC
EMPOWERMENT
INCREASING
INCOMES
GROWTH IN
AGRIBUSINESS
ENTREPRENEURIAL
VENTURES
WEALTH CREATION
AND NEW OPPORTUNITIES

Chapter 8: *Challenging Corruption and Censorship*

Have you ever wondered what it would be like to live in a world where your voice was constantly suppressed, and every action required approval from an unseen authority? Imagine a place where speaking out against injustices could result in severe consequences—not only for you but also for those close to you. This is the stark reality faced by countless individuals around the globe who battle corruption and censorship daily, striving to make their voices heard despite the overwhelming odds.

In this chapter, we delve into how transparency, accountability, and cryptocurrency offer practical tools to challenge these oppressive forces. By exploring real-world examples and presenting insightful perspectives, we aim to uncover the mechanisms through which these elements can empower individuals and transform societies shackled by corruption and censorship. Whether you're a newcomer to the world of digital finance or have been following these developments keenly, this exploration provides a fresh understanding of the potential paths towards a freer, more accountable future.

Importance of Transparency in Government Operations

Transparency shines as a powerful antidote to corruption. When governments operate openly, they pave the way for integrity and ethical conduct among public officials. But how exactly does transparency root out these corrupt practices? Let's explore further.

Imagine a world where decisions, actions, and the use of public funds are conducted behind closed doors. The absence of light allows corruption to flourish. In contrast, transparency means that everything from governmental expenditures to policymaking is open for public viewing. This openness functions like a protective measure, making it much harder for corruption to spread its tendrils.

A concrete example can drive this point home. Consider Sweden, a country renowned for its high levels of governmental transparency. The Public Access to Information and Secrecy Act, implemented there, allows citizens to access government documents effortlessly. This openness ensures that any misallocation of funds or unethical behavior is quickly brought to light. As a result, Sweden experiences lower levels of corruption compared to nations with more opaque systems.

Another salient example is the Right to Information Act in India, a landmark legislation passed in 2005. This act empowered Indian citizens to demand information from the government, thereby reducing bureaucratic discretion. In one notable case, transparency through this act helped uncover numerous 'ghost workers' drawing salaries without actual employment. By illuminating these shadowy corners, India made significant strides toward reducing corruption.

Transparency stands as crucial not just because it reforms governmental practices, but because it empowers citizens. With access to clear and comprehensive information, citizens can scrutinize government workings. They're better equipped to question, challenge, and demand change. This watchdog role is instrumental in holding governments accountable, keeping public servants on their toes, and discouraging corruption.

The mechanisms of transparency involve making meeting minutes, budgets, and policy decisions publicly accessible. Governments can use digital platforms to provide real-time data about various projects and expenditures. This practice not only assures citizens that their taxes are being put to good use but also fosters a culture of trust and credibility.

Yet, one must ask: why is citizen involvement so vital? The answer lies in an empowered society that participates actively in governance, leading to a virtuous cycle where transparency fosters trust. Trust, in turn, raises expectations for ethical behavior, reducing the likelihood of corrupt actions. It nurtures an environment where policies aren't born out of clandestine meetings but from public debates and consensus.

Moreover, transparency sets the stage for whistleblower protections, encouraging individuals to speak out against corruption without fear of repercussion. When people know that systems exist to protect them if they expose wrongdoings, they are more likely to come forward with information. This, in itself, acts as a deterrent, dissuading corrupt practices.

For public officials, transparency imposes a natural pressure. Knowing that their decisions and actions are subject to public scrutiny, officials are more likely to act with integrity. It becomes imperative for them to account for their actions, deliberate carefully, and justify their decisions. This environmental shift is critical in embedding ethical practices.

Let's delve deeper into the concept of ethical practices which are tied closely with transparency. When government procedures are transparent, they compel officials to adhere to high standards of conduct. There's a gap narrowed between what is done and what should be done—because the public eye is ever-watchful. Transparent systems embed just that: they normalize ethical behavior, creating blueprints for others to follow.

Furthermore, technology plays a vital role in enhancing transparency. Tools like blockchain drive an irreversible wave of transparency in governmental transactions. With blockchain, transactions are recorded in a secure, public ledger that is almost impossible to tamper with. It provides an unchangeable record accessible to all, ensuring absolute transparency.

But the story doesn't end at transparency. A seamless transition awaits into the realm of accountability, crucially highlighting how it further binds the transparency threads tightly. In the next section, we'll explore how Non-Governmental Organizations, much like governments, utilize accountability mechanisms to ensure transparent reporting and stakeholder involvement. Accountability stands not merely as an afterthought but as a continuation of the virtue initiated by transparency.

In closing this exploration of transparency, it's clear that transparency is not simply about clear glass panes through which government actions are visible. It is about building a transparent societal framework, where information flows freely, decisions are made in the open, and citizens actively participate in governance. Transparency acts as the guardian that ensures ethical conduct, trust, and integrity within governments, solidifying the foundation for a corruption-free society. Next, let's tackle accountability in NGOs, exploring how these constructs combine to combat malfeasance and promote ethical governance fostering societal trust.

Mechanisms for Ensuring Accountability in NGOs

Transparency serves as a linchpin in government operations, significantly reducing corruption's foothold. This same emphasis on transparency becomes equally critical for non-governmental organizations (NGOs) striving to hold themselves accountable and resist corruption. NGOs, akin to governments, shoulder the responsibility of being transparent in their operations to prevent misuse of their resources and authority.

NGOs must establish clear financial reporting systems as the first step towards accountability. By meticulously documenting expenditures and income, they not only provide a clear picture of financial health but also reduce the risk of financial abuses. These reports should be accessible to stakeholders, promoting a culture of openness. For example, in some successful cases, NGOs have implemented comprehensive online databases where stakeholders can review financial documents and funding sources. This openness fosters trust and ensures that funds are utilized effectively to serve the organization's mission. Such practices parallel governmental transparency initiatives, showing that clear reporting is foundational to upholding integrity in any sector.

Regular audits constitute another vital component for reinforcing NGO accountability. By subjecting their financial statements and operations to external scrutiny, NGOs can identify inconsistencies and rectify them promptly. An illustrative case is that of an international humanitarian NGO that encountered discrepancies in their financial records. By employing an independent auditor, they discovered a fraudulent scheme within their procurement process, allowing them to tighten controls and prevent future incidents. These audits work as a deterrent against corruption, affirming the organization's commitment to ethical conduct. The lessons from this example emphasize how rigorous checks are indispensable for sustaining an honest operational environment.

Stakeholder involvement in decision-making processes enhances both transparency and accountability. It is imperative for NGOs to actively engage donors, beneficiaries, and community members, providing them with a platform to voice concerns and contribute ideas. This collaborative approach not only democratizes the decision-making process but also invites diverse perspectives that can lead to more informed and effective strategies. A poignant illustration of this is seen in an environmental NGO that faced backlash from local communities over a conservation project. By organizing town hall meetings and participatory workshops, the NGO and the community developed a mutually agreeable approach that integrated local knowledge and values. This collaboration highlighted the importance of stakeholder engagement in preventing conflicts and fostering a sense of shared ownership in the NGO's mission.

Such participatory mechanisms mirror successful governmental practices where public consultations and inclusive policies spearhead transparent governance. Reflecting these practices, NGOs can fortify their operations against potential abuses and align their activities with the expectations and needs of their stakeholders.
However, implementing these accountability measures isn't devoid of challenges. NGOs often encounter funding constraints that may limit their ability to perform regular audits or facilitate stakeholder engagement activities. The pressure to report quickly to appease donors can lead to errors or oversights in financial reporting, undermining accountability efforts. Furthermore, resistance from within the organization may arise, particularly when introducing new transparency practices that disrupt the status quo.

Addressing these challenges requires a concerted effort from both NGO leadership and supporters. Leadership must prioritize transparency as a core organizational value, demonstrating commitment through strategic investments in accountability measures. Training staff and fostering a culture of openness are paramount, ensuring that everyone within the organization understands and upholds accountability principles. When confronted with resistance, communicating the benefits of accountability practices and involving staff in the decision-making process can ease transitions to more transparent and effective operational models. Collaborative efforts with other NGOs, governments, and private sectors can facilitate the sharing of best practices and resources. Partnerships can also help pool resources for things like collective audits or developing shared platforms for stakeholder engagement.

In addition to internal strategies, NGOs can advocate for policy changes that promote transparency and accountability within the sector. Engaging policymakers to create supportive environments where transparency tools are encouraged can lead to broader systemic improvements. Efforts to introduce or refine legal frameworks that set standards for transparency can not only enhance NGOs' governance but also align them with global best practices.
An ongoing commitment to learning and adapting must underpin NGOs' accountability efforts. This commitment includes continuously reviewing and updating practices as needed and embracing innovations that foster transparency. For instance, blockchain technology represents an emerging tool with the potential to revolutionize NGO operations by creating tamper-proof financial records, offering unparalleled transparency.

As NGOs increasingly recognize the imperative of accountability, the transition to clearer and more participatory governance models becomes more feasible. These practices not only strengthen NGOs' credibility but also empower them to address issues effectively, thereby ensuring their missions are fulfilled.

Moving forward, NGOs must brace for the challenges of promoting transparency in contexts often resistant to change. Upcoming discussions will delve into the bureaucratic resistance that hinders transparency efforts and explore the potential of digital tools and legal frameworks as catalysts for change. By overcoming such obstacles, NGOs and governments alike can strengthen their pursuit of transparency, ultimately enhancing good governance and societal trust.

Challenges and Solutions in Promoting Transparency in Both Sectors

NGOs have always been at the forefront of advocating for accountability, using diverse mechanisms to establish trust and transparency in their operations. Yet, despite their efforts, they often face substantial hurdles within bureaucratic structures known for inherent resistance and technological gaps. Promoting transparency remains crucial but challenging due to these systemic barriers. Many organizations continuously struggle to communicate their processes openly and clearly, as overhauling entrenched bureaucratic norms doesn't happen overnight.

This challenge presents a deeper issue: how do we advance transparency in systems developed to resist scrutiny? Standard methods like internal reviews and audits often get bogged down by gaps in technology or bureaucratic inertia. This is where digital transparency tools, such as blockchain-based systems, significantly show their potential. Blockchain, for example, offers a decentralized method of recording information that guarantees data immutability and real-time availability. Imagine a digital ledger shared across multiple nodes, where every transaction or decision in an organization gets recorded permanently. This creates a trusted log accessible to all stakeholders, potentially transforming how accountability operates.

The adoption of blockchain technology in government and NGOs can revolutionize transparency, moving from opaque administrative processes to fully transparent operations. By having an immutable record of every transaction, decision, and regulatory change, these tools eliminate the possibility of records being altered or erased, thereby reinforcing trust among beneficiaries and donors. They provide a clear line of sight into governmental transactions, reducing the opportunities for corrupt practices that feed off untraceable activities. Countries like Estonia have already embraced blockchain to some extent in their governance models, showing an increase in public trust and a reduction in corruption through open data and e-governance initiatives.

Legal frameworks complement these technological advancements by mandating open governance and accountability. For instance, countries in the European Union have implemented General Data Protection Regulation (GDPR) measures, prioritizing transparency and accountability. This legal backing ensures institutions are not only encouraged but bound to uphold transparency. Similarly, in 2013, the Indian government enacted the Right to Information Act, which has significantly empowered citizens by providing them with tools to demand transparency from public offices, leading to notable drops in reported corruption cases.

Despite these advances, implementing digital transparency systems isn't without challenges. Resistance from established bureaucracies is a significant barrier—those who thrive in closed environments resist disruptive changes threatening their status quo. Additionally, resource constraints can limit the broad implementation of new technologies. Developing nations, for instance, may find it difficult to allocate necessary funds towards digitalization or may lack the infrastructure needed to support such technologies.

Furthermore, the practical execution of technological solutions encounters skepticism about digital literacy and data privacy. Questions often arise about the safety and reliability of these systems. Common misconceptions need addressing to foster broader acceptance, such as clarifying how blockchain does not allow users to operate anonymously in ways that compromise accountability. Instead, it records activities publicly while protecting personal and sensitive information from exposure.

Engaging communities and stakeholders in understanding the potential benefits of transparency tools remains imperative in overcoming these hurdles. By demystifying the technology and addressing concerns head-on, governments and NGOs can foster environments more conducive to open, transparent operations. Correcting misconceptions ensures resistance diminishes over time, particularly as digital literacy increases.

At the heart of these discussions lies another burgeoning opportunity for enhancing freedom through cryptocurrency. Unlike conventional financial systems, which can easily be manipulated or surveilled, cryptocurrency offers a more private, secure form of transaction, especially vital for activists, journalists, and dissidents in regions where freedom of expression is under threat. Through privacy-preserving transactions, these groups can transfer funds without fearing exposure or retaliation from oppressive regimes. This shift to financial systems that eschew excessive oversight empowers individuals to speak more freely, encouraging a landscape where expression isn't stifled by financial manipulation.
Transitioning from transparency tools to cryptocurrency isn't just a technological upgrade—it's a profound ideological shift. It symbolizes a move towards greater individual empowerment and autonomy in a world where freedom of expression hangs in delicate balance. The groundwork laid by advances in accountability and transparency is preparatory for understanding the profound impact cryptocurrencies are having and will continue to have.

As we look to cryptocurrency's growing role in providing financial privacy and fostering expression, the conversation naturally progresses to security and empowerment in digital age activism. It's a discussion becoming increasingly relevant as more individuals seek alternatives to traditional financial systems that align more closely with their values of openness and freedom. Understanding this transition is key to appreciating how technology reshapes societal and individual dynamics and why it’s essential for us to adapt to these changes.

This seamless narrative from enhancing transparency to facilitating freedom through cryptocurrency sets the stage for deeper exploration into how these technologies combined are shaping modern governance and societal norms. They remind us not just of what is possible but of what should be pursued in the ongoing quest for a freer, more accountable future.

Role of Cryptocurrency in Enhancing Freedom of Expression and Privacy
Efforts to promote transparency often meet resistance, especially within bureaucratic systems that thrive on opacity. Digital transparency tools and new legal frameworks have emerged as crucial in addressing these challenges, yet they face formidable obstacles. For instance, bureaucratic resistance manifests in delaying tactics, convoluted processes, or outright refusal to adapt to transparency demands. These issues underscore the need for mechanisms that operate outside traditional systems, which is where cryptocurrency enters the picture.

Cryptocurrency holds potential as a privacy-preserving tool that supports transparency by enabling secure, private transactions circumventing traditional barriers. Most digital currencies utilize blockchain technology, which provides an immutable ledger, ensuring all transactions remain transparent to any interested party while preserving the anonymity of participants. Privacy-conscious narratives often focus on the negative aspects—hiding illicit activities, for instance—but for activists, journalists, and dissenters, privacy can be life-saving.

Consider a journalist operating in a regime known for its intolerance toward critical media. This journalist, reliant on donations to continue their work, faces the constant threat of government interference, financial censorship, or worse, personal harm. Here, cryptocurrency steps in as a viable alternative. It ensures the journalist can receive funds from international supporters without leaving a breadcrumb trail leading back to them. Privacy-enhancing cryptocurrencies, such as Monero or Zcash, provide robust shields against unwarranted scrutiny, facilitating ongoing operations free from the constraints of the hostile environment they operate in.

Similarly, activists operating under oppressive regimes often face financial monitoring intended to stifle dissent. By using decentralized financial systems, they bypass these obstacles. In Egypt, following the Arab Spring, activists turned to Bitcoin to fund projects without alerting government agencies notorious for clamping down on dissenters. Cryptocurrency served not just as a financial lifeline but also as a means to uphold their right to free expression without attracting the undue attention their government's presence often brings.

Cryptocurrency also serves a dual role when it comes to freedom of expression. Beyond being a tool for financial transactions, it operates as a protective mechanism against censorship. Take, for example, a non-profit organization advocating for free speech in a country where such discourse can lead to imprisonment. Traditional funding models are not feasible, for they risk alerting state actors or being blocked. By opting to use cryptocurrencies, these organizations not only maintain operations discreetly but can also ensure their work, messages, and campaigns reach the global audience, untempered by localized restrictions.

This dynamic becomes evident in Venezuela, a country grappling with severe economic instability and a government tightly gripping its populace's expression rights. Here, organizations use cryptocurrency to fundraise and spread information internationally, sidestepping state-controlled currencies and finance systems. This example highlights how cryptocurrencies empower individuals and organizations to challenge these corrupt systems, providing an avenue not just for monetary value exchange, but for preserving the critical narratives publicized amid regional turbulence.

The benefits, however, are not without challenges. Utilizing cryptocurrency requires a baseline understanding of digital currency dynamics, which might be daunting for some advocates or organizations not technologically inclined. Furthermore, not all cryptocurrencies guarantee the privacy required, with only a handful adequately serving this purpose. There is also the risk of potential government retaliation as authorities adapt, learning to track transactions and mitigate the freedom digital currencies afford.

International examples continue showcasing the power of these digital economies. In China, where stringent regulations govern financial transactions, cryptocurrencies provide citizens with financial freedom otherwise not possible. They offer a way to support independent media and initiatives that promote free speech, navigating around state-imposed restrictions that would otherwise suppress such efforts.

In Iran, another regime noted for censorship and financial control, citizens resort to Bitcoin as a hedge against economic uncertainty while ensuring their transactions avoid governmental oversight. This scenario reflects a broader global trend, where in several nations, authoritarianism presents digital finance not just as a tool, but sometimes as a necessity for independent media and social change leaders to continue operating effectively.

Yet, the challenge remains: how to ensure the benefits of cryptocurrency can be universally accessed without compromising safety or privacy. This issue calls for education and advocacy, ensuring the pivotal players in the sphere of human rights understand and harness digital currencies' full potential. More so, it demands global cooperation to devise regulations that protect individual freedoms without undermining the technology's rising prevalence as a form of liberation from governmental control.

Cryptocurrencies' ability to bypass censorship and bolster individual rights sets the stage for discussions on their wider applications. Beyond protecting journalists and activists, they fund initiatives promoting free speech, especially in countries where speaking out can cost lives. As we delve further into these realms, understanding their dual capability as both a financial instrument and a form of expression will enable its broader acceptance and integration in combating global censorship efforts. The ensuing dialogue explores how these currencies can enhance expression and secure an uncensored future for all.

Examples of How Crypto is Used to Bypass Censorship and Protect Individual Rights

Cryptocurrency, with its promise of privacy, emerges as a powerful ally for those fighting censorship and corruption. By allowing transactions that protect identities, cryptocurrency offers activists, journalists, and dissidents a means of financial freedom that traditional systems often deny them. This aspect isn't just a technicality; it's a lifeline for individuals operating under repressive regimes where dissent is dangerous. When facing governments that monitor conventional financial transactions, the privacy built into cryptocurrencies ensures these individuals can continue their essential work without undue risk of exposure.

In societies where governments wield censorship as a tool of control, cryptocurrencies afford a rare opportunity to bypass oppressive financial oversight. Their decentralized nature allows for transactions that are not only private but also resistant to government interference. This makes cryptocurrencies invaluable for funding independent media, supporting free speech initiatives, and backing movements that challenge oppressive narratives. By offering financial independence, cryptocurrency empowers individuals and groups to speak out and share information in environments where traditional funding sources can't reach.

Examples around the globe illustrate how cryptocurrencies support free speech and combat censorship. In Venezuela, for instance, amid economic collapse and government mismanagement, cryptocurrencies provide a means for citizens to navigate the country's hyperinflation. Here, digital currencies not only preserve purchasing power but also facilitate international transactions relatively free from government intervention. This helps activists and independent media maintain operations within a restrictive landscape.

Similarly, in countries like Iran, facing international sanctions and economic isolation, cryptocurrency presents an alternative financial system. Citizens and businesses use it to circumvent restrictive banking systems, allowing for continued trade and exchange where traditional methods have failed. By operating outside governmental controls, cryptocurrencies offer a glimmer of hope in harsh economic climates. They promote transparency and accountability by highlighting discrepancies and providing a means to expose financial misreporting or curtail corrupt practices.

Transparency through blockchain technology offers a practical solution for holding entities accountable. When transactions are recorded on a decentralized ledger visible to all, it becomes challenging for organizations to conceal misconduct. Cryptocurrencies enable citizens and watchdog organizations to track financial flows, ensuring that resources are used appropriately and highlighting any irregularities. This transparency acts as a deterrent against corruption. Organizations or governments aware of increased scrutiny are less likely to engage in corrupt practices.

Consider Uganda, where cryptocurrency donations hold potential in offsetting government corruption. By channeling funds directly to projects and communities through blockchain, donors can ensure their contributions reach intended recipients

without falling prey to corrupt officials. This model, while not without its challenges, symbolizes a shift towards greater financial transparency and accountability, making corruption more difficult to conceal.
Moreover, cryptocurrencies redefine how democratic initiatives receive funding. Traditional methods often involve rigid regulations and susceptibility to political influence, which restrict funding flows. Cryptocurrencies bypass these barriers, empowering democratic movements and organizations to secure funding from global supporters without interference. The immutable nature of blockchain ensures each transaction is verifiable and accountable, preventing misallocation.

In Myanmar, following the military coup, citizens turned to cryptocurrencies as a safe haven from the rapidly devaluing local currency. Through digital transactions, activists and dissidents funded campaigns advocating for democracy and human rights. These contributions occurred largely outside the purview of the controlling junta, highlighting how cryptocurrencies can sustain democratic practices even amidst authoritarian governance.
Furthermore, cryptocurrencies facilitate the dissemination of information in environments strangleheld by censorship. When governments attempt to silence dissenting voices, cryptocurrency-financed platforms ensure information continues circulating. This was evident during the Arab Spring, where activists used encrypted digital currencies to support servers hosting revolutionary content outside state control. In doing so, cryptocurrencies helped dismantle digital firewalls that authoritarian regimes erect to quell rebellion.
This intersection between cryptocurrency and freedom is no accident; rather, it arises from shared values. Both prioritize decentralization and transparency, cornerstones of democratic governance. Cryptocurrency, by its design, resists central control and promotes individual empowerment. This aligns seamlessly with principles that underpin democratic societies: the free flow of information, accountability, and protection against unjust dominance.

It's crucial, however, to acknowledge the double-edged nature of cryptocurrencies. While offering tools against oppression, they can also be manipulated by malicious actors for illegal activities. Mitigating this requires striking a balance: strengthening the benefits of cryptocurrencies for democratic ends while implementing safeguards against misuse. Clear regulations and international cooperation remain vital to ensure cryptocurrencies remain tools for good rather than conduits for harm.
A holistic, nuanced understanding of cryptocurrency's role against censorship involves recognizing its potential to disrupt corrupt systems. Through transparency, it curtails corruption's power, empowering citizens to demand accountability. By enabling unhindered information dissemination, it combats censorship, ensuring voices remain undiminished even in the most repressive environments.

Cryptocurrency's potential to redefine interactions with oppressive regimes can't be overstated. It embodies hope for those striving towards liberty and justice, driving a shift towards transparency and empowerment. But realizing this potential requires vigilance. We must foster environments where cryptocurrencies' positives flourish while curbing negative aspects. This involves ongoing dialogue and cooperative efforts, ensuring cryptocurrencies contribute positively to society.

As we continue exploring the cryptocurrency's revolutionary promise, it's essential to engage with its complexities. The technology offers freedom, but responsibly channeling it against censorship and corruption needs global commitment. By leveraging cryptocurrencies wisely, we can promote transparency, accountability, and freedom, ensuring a brighter, more equitable future.

Final Insights

As we wrap up this chapter, the exploration of transparency, accountability, and cryptocurrency within governments and NGOs unveils a transformative potential in combating corruption and censorship. By embracing these tools, societies can initiate a profound shift towards open governance, allowing citizens to hold their leaders accountable and fostering trust through clear information sharing. Cryptocurrency offers an innovative pathway for financial privacy and freedom, empowering individuals in oppressive regions to operate independently of restrictive regimes. Now that we understand these powerful mechanisms, we can envision a future where ethical practices and citizen engagement thrive, leading to more transparent, equitable societies. With continued collaboration and adaptation, these technologies can redefine governance and empower individuals globally, paving the way for a brighter, more inclusive future.

Chapter 9: *Redefining Work and Earning*

Picture a world where your professional commitments no longer tie you to one desk, one city, or even one country. Imagine having the freedom to choose when and how you work, dictated not by an office schedule but by personal passion and financial goals. This isn't just a fantasy borne out of wishful thinking; it's a reality reshaping how we view work and earnings today. As technology evolves, it ushers in a new era defined by flexibility and choice—one that challenges the traditional nine-to-five grind and presents a landscape ripe with opportunity and uncertainty alike.

In this chapter, we'll venture into how the gig economy redefines our understanding of work, delve into the rise of freelancing as a viable career path, explore how borderless payments make global transactions seamless, and examine the burgeoning digital art economies powered by NFTs. Join us as we unpack these transformative elements, offering insights into the seismic shift redefining labor and income in a world rapidly moving towards more dynamic and diverse economic models.

The Gig Economy

The gig economy, a term you're likely familiar with, describes a labor market characterized by short-term contracts or freelance work as opposed to permanent jobs. At its core, it thrives on flexibility, autonomy, and the freedom for workers to choose when and where they work. In recent years, platforms have sprung up to facilitate this type of work, disrupting traditional employment models and offering alternatives that are attractive to a growing number of individuals.

Take Uber and Lyft, for example. They've revolutionized the transportation sector by offering drivers a way to earn money on their terms. Drivers sign in when they want, operate on their schedules, and decide how much or how little they want to work each week. This setup contrasts sharply with the fixed schedules and commitments of conventional taxi drivers. Similarly, Airbnb has reshaped accommodation, allowing homeowners to rent out spaces on a flexible basis, appealing to those who prefer a less rigid approach to earning from property.

The idea of short-term engagements isn't new, but technology has amplified its reach. Gig platforms make it possible to connect those offering services with those seeking them on a global scale. Upwork and Fiverr epitomize this capability by bringing together freelancers from various fields—graphic design, writing, programming—with clients worldwide. This model not only broadens the potential client base for freelancers but also encourages people to pursue work that matches their skills and interest without getting tethered to a single employer.

A key driver behind the gig economy's allure is the shift in work preferences, especially among millennials and younger generations. Many seek a balance between work and personal life, valuing experiences and flexibility over traditional job success metrics. The gig economy accommodates these desires by allowing them to pick projects based on interest and availability, diverging from the nine-to-five grind.

However, this flexibility doesn't come without its drawbacks. While gig work empowers individuals, allowing for control over one's professional life and decisions, it also raises important questions about job security and long-term benefits. Many gig workers operate as independent contractors, meaning they do not receive traditional employment benefits like health insurance, retirement plans, or paid leave. This ambiguity in employment status can be a significant trade-off for the independence and autonomy that the gig economy promises.

Consider the case of a freelance graphic designer in New York. On platforms like Fiverr, they can choose projects that suit their creative interests, setting their rates and managing their time. This system allows them to work on diverse assignments for different clients simultaneously, avoiding stagnancy and keeping their portfolio dynamic. Yet, without employer-provided insurance, they must manage their healthcare independently, weighing the costs against their earnings.

Studies indicate that a significant percentage of gig workers appreciate their independence and the ability to earn supplementary income. A Pew Research study reflects how side hustles have become synonymous with financial freedom for some, cushioning against full reliance on traditional employment. But it’s worth mentioning that not every gig worker is part of the economy by choice—many are driven by necessity, finding themselves in between jobs or needing extra income.

Platforms like TaskRabbit further illustrate the evolving job roles in the gig economy. They connect users who need odd jobs done—like assembling furniture or home repairs—with individuals willing to complete these tasks, essentially turning a casual skill into a moneymaking opportunity without the commitment of a full-time job. Workers gain exposure to varied tasks and clients, enhancing their skill set, which can be highly beneficial for those seeking to explore different fields or industries.

Even so, the question of how to ensure fair compensation and protection for gig workers remains unresolved. Advocacy for policies that recognize gig workers' contributions and vulnerabilities has gained momentum. Employment laws and regulations struggle to keep pace with this swiftly changing landscape, often leaving gig workers in a gray area without the same legal protections as traditional employees.

As you think about what's driving these changes, consider the role technology plays in redefining work and professional stability. It’s not only gig workers who are riding this wave; freelancers are finding newer ways to anchor flexibility within a more structured framework. The rise of digital tools and platforms has enabled them to segment their traditional job functions into freelance gigs, offering a way to sustain flexible careers while maintaining a degree of financial and professional stability that gig work alone might not afford.

This transition brings us to the broader freelancing movement. Unlike purely gig-based work, freelancing often involves longer-term projects and client relationships, sometimes providing a more consistent income stream. Technological advancements empower freelancers to carve out niche areas of expertise, enhance their portfolios digitally, and tap into global markets without the restrictions of geographical boundaries. It’s a concept offering depth in career diversification and stimulating innovation within industries.

As you let these ideas simmer, prepare for an exploration into how freelancers, utilizing technology, contribute to evolving industries. You’ll see how they redefine stability through digital tools and creative ventures, disrupting and transforming professional landscapes while embracing new opportunities in a dynamic economy.

Rise of Freelancers

The gig economy has already challenged traditional work models, shaking the foundations of the nine-to-five job and introducing a new era of employment flexibility. With the emergence of freelancers, the concept of work has been transformed into something dynamic and fluid. This shift marks an evolution from the conventional employment structures where stability meant a steady paycheck and a retirement plan. Now, flexibility has become a key element of modern work life, offering opportunities that were previously inaccessible in such a liberated form.

Freelancers are at the forefront of this transition. They're reshaping industries by embracing flexible engagements that rely heavily on the advancements of technology. The notion of having a singular career path from start to finish is becoming obsolete, as individuals tap into diverse opportunities provided by freelance work. It's no longer about finding a job within commuting distance—it's about finding the right job, even if it's on another continent. This new landscape allows individuals to carve out unique careers, marked by creativity and adaptability.

The rise of freelancing has introduced a new paradigm of stability, even if it doesn't come with the traditional trappings of job security. Freelancers navigate the complexities of unpredictable income and the hustle of securing new clients with a sense of autonomy that many conventional jobs simply cannot match. The sense of empowerment they gain often outweighs the uncertainty they face. Freelancers have a level of control over their professional lives that allows them to configure their careers according to personal priorities and lifestyle choices.

In the broader context of how people work and earn, the significance of this shift cannot be overstated. It highlights a pivotal facet of the ongoing transformation in employment structures, emphasizing the increased need for fluidity and personal agency in work arrangements. The move towards freelancing is only the beginning, as development in global finance, like borderless payments, presents even more opportunities for freelancers on the worldwide stage.

Industries like graphic design, writing, software development, and digital marketing are being profoundly impacted by the rise of freelancers. These sectors thrive on creativity and innovation and are particularly well-suited to the independent contractor model. In the graphics design world, the demand for unique and original content allows freelancers to continually find work across different platforms, catering to a variety of commercial clients. As a result, businesses gain access to a diverse talent pool without the overhead costs associated with full-time employees.

Writing and content creation have similarly evolved, with freelancers crafting articles, stories, and marketing content for a global audience. This demand for tailored storytelling and engaging narratives ensures a constant stream of opportunities for freelance writers. Bloggers can transform their unique voices into recognizable personal brands while ghostwriters supply their skills to those requiring content but lacking time or expertise.

Software development is another field where freelance talent is in high demand. Startups and even established tech companies increasingly benefit from bringing on developers who can work on specific projects, facilitating cost-effectiveness and agility that a permanent team might not provide. This flexibility allows companies to scale quickly and efficiently without compromising on the quality of their output.

Digital marketing is yet another thriving arena for freelancers. In an age where digital presence is crucial, companies of all sizes need experts who can navigate online platforms to effectively engage and grow their consumer base. Freelancers offer this specialized knowledge and adaptability, catering campaigns to match a brand's specific needs.

The advancement in technology is the catalyst that propels freelancers onto the global stage. Platforms such as Upwork, Fiverr, and Freelancer enable independent workers to connect with clients worldwide. Freelancers are not just limited to their local markets anymore; they possess the ability to engage with a global client base, using digital tools and remote communication to overcome geographical limitations.

For businesses, hiring freelancers provides a path to achieving cost efficiencies. Companies can access talented professionals for specific projects without the long-term financial commitment of a full-time employee. This allows businesses to remain lean and adaptable, a significant advantage in rapidly changing markets. The diversity of thought and cultural backgrounds that freelancers bring can also lead to richer, more innovative solutions tailored to a variety of markets and audiences.

As we begin to understand the full scale of this transformation in how work and earnings are perceived, the role of borderless payments becomes evident. Financial innovations like crypto and digital payment systems lower barriers for freelancers, enabling seamless, cross-border transactions. This evolution in how money transfer is handled further empowers freelancers, allowing them to work from anywhere in the world without worrying about logistics.

These financial tools facilitate transactions across continents and time zones, minimizing delays and currency conversion issues that often accompany international freelancing. It's a significant step toward a more globalized work environment where talent can flow freely and efficiently, no matter where it originates. This has ushered in an era where the physical location of work has become irrelevant, provided one has a stable internet connection and the necessary skills.

As we transition to discuss borderless payments in greater detail, consider how they continue to revolutionize the freelance landscape. These systems are pushing the envelope, making freelancing a more viable and attractive option for talented individuals worldwide. The implications of these evolutions in payments are crucial to fostering an environment where freelance work not only thrives but continues to expand beyond previous limitations. Embracing these changes brings new opportunities, breaking down walls and building bridges in the ever-evolving landscape of global work and earnings.

Subpoint 3: Borderless Payments

Freelancers are reshaping industries by using technology to build diverse careers. They've moved away from the traditional 9-to-5 grind, instead opting for more flexible arrangements that align with personal goals and preferences. Technology offers freelancers tools to reach global markets, turning the entire planet into potential business partners and clients. The concept of stability changes in this context. No longer does it mean staying with one company for decades; instead, it's about creating a portfolio of varied opportunities, ready to pivot as demands change.

Here's where borderless payments enter the scene. For freelancers, getting paid is a global affair, requiring tools that transcend geographic and banking boundaries. These financial technologies support seamless cross-border transactions, giving freelancers the autonomy to work wherever they find opportunity, unconstrained by their physical location or local banking limitations. For example, services like PayPal, Payoneer, and Wise have revolutionized how freelancers get paid. They allow instantaneous currency exchange and provide the ability to send and receive money in various currencies without exorbitant fees. This ease of financial movement is transformative in today's world of online work.

Think about it: a freelance graphic designer in India can serve clients in the United States or Europe without the logistical nightmares of yesteryear. Payments can be made in multiple currencies, swiftly and securely, ensuring that freelancers can manage an international client base without losing a significant portion of their income to fees or lengthy banking processes. Not only does this allow freelancers to earn from countries with stronger currencies, but it also opens up the playing field for them to compete on a global level. Borderless payments level the playing field by making it feasible to conduct transactions worldwide.

Consider also the impact on small businesses that hire freelancers. They now have access to talent from around the globe. Companies no longer need to be in proximity to top-tier talent, allowing them to assemble diverse and skilled teams without geographical limitations. This access provides a competitive edge as they can quickly adapt to market changes by hiring experts from different regions who bring unique perspectives and approaches.

While many consider borderless payments a solution for high-profile gigs or tech-related jobs, they extend further into various fields. Writers, marketers, educators, and virtually any profession imaginable can benefit. Social media influencers, for instance, can work with advertisers from different countries, expanding their reach and audience. By overcoming geographical barriers, borderless payments enable workers to connect with the world, transforming potential clients into real revenue sources.

This speaks to a broader shift towards an interconnected global workforce. Freelancers have the tools necessary to thrive wherever they can build their niche. Language barriers and time zones might remain challenges, but the primary hurdle of financial transaction capability has been addressed fully with these technologies. This creates a more inclusive economic environment, where irrespective of location, people can collaborate and innovate together.

Additionally, the trust factor in financial transactions has drastically improved with borderless payment solutions. These platforms often come with built-in protections against fraud, ensuring secure transactions between international clients and freelancers. Ratings, reviews, and histories of account holders provide transparency, helping to build trust between parties and encouraging more users to engage in global work.

One intriguing aspect is the empowerment of individuals in economically restricted regions. Freelancers in underdeveloped countries can access economic opportunities previously unavailable. With internet access, they can learn, improve upon skills, and connect with global companies that want their services. A programmer in Nigeria could contribute code to a startup in San Francisco without worrying about how they'll receive payment, thus enabling a meaningful exchange of skills and services.

Critically examining these developments paints a picture of transformation where finance and work are concerned. Borderless payments are a piece of the financial puzzle that supports the gig economy's continued growth and freelancers' central role in global economies. The trend demonstrates a shift in work culture reflecting flexibility, adaptability, and resilience, where traditional employment models get left behind in favor of more dynamic, tech-supported options.

As we pivot toward the next frontier of digital commerce, it's worthwhile to note that while borderless payments are one cog in the machine, they are essential for the whole system to function. Freelancers have not only adapted to this but also embraced it, seeing larger earnings and more fluid career paths because of these capabilities.

Our exploration of borderless payments clearly outlines how they serve as a backbone for freelance work. By enabling this pivotal shift in financial and work practices, freelancers are better positioned to capitalize on global markets and contribute uniquely to the global economy. While discussing financial flows, this innovation inevitably intersects with others, like Non-Fungible Tokens (NFTs) revolutionizing the digital economy.

The upcoming section will delve into how NFTs give creators unprecedented opportunities to monetize digital creations. They make it possible for digital artists, graphic designers, and content creators to attach value to their work in ways previously thought impossible. This evolution offers a new dimension of digital work and earning, distinct from the traditional models we've examined. While borderless payments have helped freelancers engage globally, NFTs present an intriguing avenue for diversifying and enhancing potential digital revenue streams. Together, these innovations shape the narrative of a digitally interconnected world where traditional definitions of work and earnings begin to blur.

NFTs and Creators

As global freelance opportunities expand, borderless payments come into play, erasing geographical constraints and sparking unprecedented creative collaborations among artists and freelancers worldwide. We now venture into the bustling world of NFTs, which have emerged as a beacon of innovation for digital creators seeking new ways to monetize their art. These digital tokens have transformed the landscape by providing a platform for artists to showcase and sell their work in a medium that security, transparency, and traceability back.

NFTs, or Non-Fungible Tokens, have rapidly gained attention for their potential to revolutionize the digital art economy. Artists who previously struggled to gain recognition and secure financial compensation for their digital creations now have avenues to generate income on a global scale. This new form of ownership allows creators to link a piece of digital art with a unique code on the blockchain, thereby establishing a digital "original" with verifiable authenticity. For artists, this means shifting from the traditional art sale methods, where only a single or limited number of originals exist, to a model where infinite ownership variants can spark interest and engagement. The allure of NFTs lies in their ability to engage diverse audiences. Crypto enthusiasts, local and international investors, and art connoisseurs find a common ground where the value of art and digital ownership intersects. The NFT market offers a unique blend of creativity and investment potential that resonates across various sectors. This crossover appeal, combined with the innate scarcity and exclusivity inherent in NFT investments, creates a dynamic environment for both creators and collectors.

Concrete examples illustrate this transformative potential. Consider Beeple, a digital artist whose work fetched an astounding $69 million at auction, catapulting the concept of NFT art into the mainstream. This success demonstrated the significant financial opportunities available within the NFT ecosystem. The story of Pak, another digital artist who embraced NFTs, further exemplifies this shift. Pak's creations, characterized by their simplicity and varying editions, provide a different artistic value proposition: affordability. Having raised over a million dollars through multiple NFT sales, Pak maintains a balance between exclusivity and accessibility, effectively sating the appetite of a diverse range of collectors.

This success is not limited to high-profile cases. Emerging artists have also seized the opportunity to carve out their niches within the NFT market. By leveraging online platforms such as OpenSea, Rarible, and Foundation, creators access global audiences and compete on equal footing with more established names in art. NFTs ensure that each artwork retains its unique identity, and creators can establish perpetual royalties every time their pieces change hands in the secondary market. This aspect enables artists to benefit financially from the appreciation of their work over time, a luxury not afforded by traditional sales.

As the NFT trend continues its upward trajectory, individual artists navigate this market to communicate their stories and engage audiences meaningfully. Personal branding and social media presence grow increasingly important, allowing creators to establish direct connections with potential buyers and supporters. The proliferation of these digital networks helps cultivate a strong sense of community among artists, collectors, and enthusiasts, further fueling the NFT marketplace's growth.

Moreover, NFTs lower the barriers to entry for aspiring artists who might not have a platform to showcase their talent. Without the constraints of traditional gallery exhibitions and gatekeepers, creators can freely express themselves and experiment with various digital formats, including video, music, and interactive media. This shift democratizes the art world, instigating an influx of diverse perspectives and narratives challenging conventional norms.

While the NFT ecosystem remains in its nascent stages, industries across the entertainment spectrum are starting to take notice. Musicians, filmmakers, and game developers recognize the potential of NFTs to not only redefine monetization models but also foster deeper connections with their audiences. The decentralized nature of blockchain technology empowers creators across disciplines to experiment with value distribution methods that honor the preferences and intentions of both artists and patrons.

As the conversation surrounding digital art and technological advancements continues to grow more robust, attention inevitably turns to the underlying blockchain infrastructure that supports NFTs. The decentralized ledger captures every transaction, providing an indelible record of provenance and authenticity. This rekindles an appreciation for ownership and originality, previously diluted by infinite digital replicability. By aligning creative output with an almost untamable digital marketplace, artists explore unprecedented avenues for their work to gain traction and value.

This brings us to the edge of the digital art revolution. In the next section, we delve deeper into how digital ownership and blockchain technology catalyze reinvention in the art world. The seamless weaving of creativity and technology challenges preconceived notions of value, sparking conversations centered around disruption and evolution. As we transition into this new realm; we uncover how these forces reshape not only how we create and consume art but perceive its significance within a rapidly changing global landscape.

Digital Art Revolution

NFTs are transforming the digital art world in groundbreaking ways, reshaping the landscape for artists across the globe. Before diving into this section's focus, it's vital to acknowledge their profound impact on creators and the digital economy. Artists now monetize their work and engage with audiences like never before, laying the groundwork for a revolution in how we perceive and value art.

Consider an artist who can now mint a digital artwork as an NFT. This token verifies its uniqueness on the blockchain, providing indisputable proof of authenticity and ownership. This process opens new doors for artists who previously struggled with fears of plagiarism and unauthorized use of their work. Digitally savvy artists find themselves empowered in an age where ownership had become nebulous. Think of Masao Ota, a Japanese digital artist whose work focused on striking digital landscapes. Before NFTs, his work often circulated uncredited on the internet. NFTs allowed him to reclaim ownership, secure his works, and receive deserved recognition. Each sale of his NFT results in immediate compensation, a novel leap from past challenges where payment depended on galleries or other intermediaries.

In the world of traditional art, provenance—or the history of ownership—ensures authenticity and boosts value. Yet, provenance was elusive in the digital sphere until NFTs emerged. Blockchain technology tracks transactions in a decentralized ledger, ensuring a detailed history of each artwork. This development not only increases trust but also allows potential buyers to trace the chain of ownership with unprecedented ease. Consider an artist like Vanessa Goldman, whose digital creations explore urban life through vivid color palettes. Each piece she creates becomes an NFT, with her initial sale establishing its base value. As her work changes hands, blockchain maintains an immutable track record, enhancing its market confidence.

Additionally, royalties have become a reality for artists with NFTs. Traditional art transactions rarely included provisions for artists to benefit from secondary sales, but the blockchain allows creators to set terms that grant them a percentage of profits from any future resale. This revolutionary change means artists aren't just compensated once, but continue to earn as their work appreciates in value and changes ownership. Take, for instance, the rising star, Rafael Montenegro. When Montenegro released his vibrant abstract pieces as NFTs, he programmed a 10% royalty into their smart contracts on the blockchain. This move ensured a continuous source of revenue as his work's popularity soared, allowing him to invest in new projects and sustain his career. Moreover, the accessibility of global platforms for selling NFTs further reshapes how art is distributed and consumed. Artists now reach audiences worldwide without the limitations of traditional art markets. NFT marketplaces like OpenSea and Rarible provide platforms for artists to showcase their talents to global collectors, enabling direct artist-to-buyer transactions. This shift democratizes the art world, emphasizing artistic merit over connections or geographic barriers. Artists from locations as varied as Buenos Aires to Bangalore find themselves interacting with collectors from all corners of the globe, enriching their creative exposure and opportunities.

Blockchain's immutable nature also challenges the perception of artistic value. Digital art's arguable lack of "uniqueness" and "scarcity" is revisited under NFTs. Every NFT is unique, underscoring digital art's distinctiveness and fostering a shift in how value is constructed. While traditional art collectors may value the tangibility of a painting or sculpture, NFT advocates argue that the digital medium's reproducibility paradoxically emphasizes rather than diminishes its worth due to secure ownership and verified authenticity. For example, a digital artist crafting a mesmerizing, generative art piece can mint it as an NFT, offering the assurance that this digital creation, while potentially replicable in appearance, is truly singular in its blockchain-verified existence.

Critics may argue that NFTs' environmental impact cannot be overlooked, as blockchain transactions carry a significant carbon footprint. However, shifts towards more sustainable technologies, like Ethereum's anticipated transition to a proof-of-stake model, aim to address these concerns. Artists committed to eco-friendly practices already seek ways to minimize their carbon footprints. They explore collaboration with environmentally-conscious platforms, highlighting a priority aligned with global sustainability efforts. This movement illustrates how the digital art revolution does not operate in isolation but aligns with broader cultural and environmental shifts.
Lastly, the ubiquity of NFTs prompts a reevaluation of what art "ownership" means in the digital age. In contrast to merely possessing a tangible object, NFT ownership encompasses holding a digital asset that can live on an array of devices, viewed across continents, reflecting how our engagement with art extends into virtual domains. The NFT movement offers individuals a modern means to collect, own, and display art in diverse, innovative ways, beyond the confines of physical space. This evolution mirrors a broader shift toward digital integration in our lives, where owning a digital masterpiece carries as much weight and cultural significance as possessing a traditional painting. Analyzing NFTs' impacts allows us to see how digital ownership and blockchain technology shape creativity, artistic value, and artists' roles in a global context. This evolution might represent one of the most profound shifts within our modern cultural fabric. The digital art revolution continues, challenging traditional concepts and inviting fresh perspectives on art's potential in our ever-evolving digital tapestry.

Concluding Thoughts
As we've explored, the transformation of work and earnings through the gig economy, freelancing, borderless payments, and digital art economies is reshaping how we engage with our careers and financial opportunities. This shift disrupts traditional employment models, offering newfound flexibility and global connectivity. Gig workers enjoy autonomy, while freelancers leverage technology to access worldwide markets without geographical constraints. Borderless payment systems enable these global interactions, allowing seamless transactions across borders, which in turn democratizes the freelance market, breaking down entry barriers for individuals in developing regions. As NFTs revolutionize the digital art landscape, artists and creators can monetize their work securely and transparently on a global scale. With these advancements, we're poised to continue evolving our understanding of work and income—an evolution that signals vast potential for reinvention across industries. Now that we've grasped these transformative dynamics, there lies an exciting opportunity to harness this new era of work, fostering creativity and economic empowerment across diverse fields and communities worldwide.

Chapter 10: Education and Financial Literacy

Education and Financial Literacy

Jake had always been fascinated by technology, but like many, he was wary of cryptocurrencies. He'd overheard conversations about Bitcoin at work and read articles that tossed around terms like blockchain and DeFi, yet it all seemed too complex to tackle head-on. One evening, while trying to pay rent online, Jake faced an unexpected issue—his transaction was blocked due to a system error from his bank. Frustrated, he couldn't help but recall the ease with which his friend Marcus sent money overseas using digital currency. That quick transaction, unencumbered by banking hours or fees, piqued Jake's interest in understanding this financial frontier.

The scenario illustrates a growing curiosity and necessity among people who wish to navigate modern financial landscapes more independently. This chapter will delve into how cryptocurrencies are reshaping financial literacy and education. Whether you're just stepping into the world of crypto or seeking to integrate it into your professional sphere, we'll explore how these digital assets can simplify and enhance our understanding of finance.

Introduction to the Importance of Financial Literacy in Education and the Role of Cryptocurrencies

Financial literacy is more crucial than ever, especially in a rapidly digitizing world. Cryptocurrencies, often seen as the wild frontier of finance, offer an unparalleled opportunity to boost our understanding of money. While some view crypto as volatile or unreliable, its very nature challenges us to learn about complex financial systems through direct experience and engagement.

Cryptocurrencies force us to think differently about financial literacy. For aspiring investors and professionals, digital assets aren't just a new way to invest—they're a gateway into understanding more about how financial systems operate. Since they operate outside the traditional frameworks, they can make us more mindful of how financial systems work and why they sometimes fail. This is especially important for students and policymakers who need to grasp the fundamentals of economics and finance in an evolving digital economy.

Engaging with cryptocurrencies offers more than just a theoretical understanding of finance. It provides hands-on experience with digital transactions, blockchain technology, and decentralized finance (DeFi). These interactions can help demystify terms often cloaked in heavy jargon. Take blockchain, for instance. Rather than seeing it as a complex system full of cryptographic puzzles, engaging with it as technology simplifies the concept into something actionable: a digital ledger that enhances transparency and security.

Cryptocurrencies also introduce a fresh perspective on financial transactions. Imagine sending money to friends or family across borders within minutes, without paying high fees, or waiting for days for the transaction to process. This practical experience with digital transactions enhances our grasp of how not just cryptocurrencies, but all digital payment systems work, offering a valuable lesson on efficiency and cost-effectiveness.

Decentralized finance, or DeFi, further expands financial literacy. DeFi platforms eliminate intermediaries, making financial services accessible to anyone with an internet connection. Engaging with DeFi platforms educates users on the importance of traditional roles filled by banks, while also introducing concepts of lending, borrowing, and trading in a more direct manner. Aspiring investors can practice these financial activities first-hand, fostering a deeper understanding of interest rates, liquidity, and investment risks versus opportunities.

Cryptocurrencies also invite exploration into the protection of digital assets. Understanding private keys, digital wallets, and encryption enhances comprehension of financial security. These lessons are increasingly important as digital theft and cyber security become more pressing issues globally. Learning about securing one's digital assets naturally extends to smarter practices in managing finances, protecting data, and understanding digital privacy.

Interactive, real-world experiences with cryptocurrencies challenge traditional views of money. Crypto newcomers are often surprised to learn that it's not just about price speculation. Rather, it's about the potential for greater financial inclusion and a broader understanding of economics. Stories of once-unbanked populations using digital currencies to participate in global commerce not only inspire, they also educate. They transform abstract economic principles into tangible narratives, showing the real impact of financial literacy on people's lives.

To make these concepts even more relatable, consider smart contracts. These self-executing contracts with the terms of the agreement between buyer and seller directly written into code come to life through direct participation in the crypto world. For both everyday transactions and more complex financial deals, understanding how smart contracts cut out the middlemen offers real-world illustrations of efficiency and self-governance.

The blend of cryptocurrencies and financial literacy becomes a vibrant educational tool across various demographics. For policymakers, understanding this dynamic can help shape regulations that not only govern digital assets more effectively, but also foster innovation. Students can integrate their knowledge of digital finance into a greater understanding of global markets. For professionals, especially those in finance and technology sectors, crypto investments introduce fresh angles on asset management and financial strategies.

To provide a concrete example, consider how a learning platform might integrate cryptocurrencies into its curriculum. By using a digital token that students earn for achieving learning milestones, educators can demonstrate the principles of supply and demand, while also incentivizing learning. This practical application engages students and translates academic concepts into personal experience. Such initiatives elucidate abstract ideas about economics and finance, while simultaneously enhancing engagement with the educational material itself.

Avoiding redundancy in this discussion highlights various ways cryptocurrencies reshape our financial education landscape. Shared stories about individuals and communities adopting crypto offer varied perspectives, each adding a layer of understanding. Whether it's younger generations using digital wallets for saving or older adults embracing digital tools to better manage retirement funds, these experiences culminate in a multidimensional story of financial empowerment.

As we transition to the upcoming section, the practical experiences you're gaining through engagement with cryptocurrencies pave the way for a deeper dive into these technologies. Prepare to explore how leveraging cryptocurrencies can enhance the understanding of traditional finance systems, offering clearer insights into previously opaque concepts. Such exploration does more than extend financial literacy; it democratizes access to financial opportunities, bridging gaps and fostering inclusion across diverse populations.

Detailed Exploration of How Crypto Technology Aids in Spreading Financial Knowledge

The previous section explored the growing importance of financial literacy in today's world. Cryptocurrencies play a significant role in this educational evolution, offering unique opportunities to engage deeply with financial concepts. Unlike traditional finance, which can often feel inaccessible and complex, cryptocurrencies provide practical experiences that are instrumental in facilitating understanding. Imagine diving into the world of finance, not through textbooks filled with dense jargon, but through interactive experiences that bring these concepts to life. This is where cryptocurrencies shine, allowing individuals to navigate and interact with blockchain, digital transactions, and decentralized finance in a hands-on manner.

Consider blockchain technology, often described as difficult but crucial to understand how it supports cryptocurrencies. Many crypto education platforms enable learners to visualize and engage with blockchain processes through interactive simulations. These tools demystify the technology by allowing individuals to see transactions unfold in real-time, illustrating how data is securely added to a chain in blocks. This demystification is all about breaking down barriers that often prevent newcomers from fully understanding financial systems.

Decentralized finance, or DeFi, offers another robust avenue for practical learning. Traditional banking can feel like a closed system for those without insider knowledge, but DeFi platforms allow users to participate in lending, borrowing, and earning interest in an open and transparent manner. Aspiring investors, professionals in finance, and educators can explore DeFi protocols, understanding their workings without a middleman. This hands-on approach can lead to a deeper appreciation for financial processes and systems forgotten or overlooked in conventional learning settings.

Furthermore, through cryptocurrencies, we find a wealth of practical applications that extend learning beyond theoretical concepts. For example, using crypto wallets provides direct engagement with securing digital assets, teaching individuals about cyber-security, responsibility, and the importance of safe digital practices. For students and educators, these are not just abstract ideas; they become vital lessons with immediate real-world application, promoting caution and awareness in digital engagements.

Education platforms have emerged, specifically targeting beginners, to offer gamified learning experiences. Think of how significantly more engaging it can be to learn through online challenges and rewards rather than dry lectures. These platforms guide users through real-world scenarios, emphasizing action over passive consumption, which is crucial in reinforcing understanding. For instance, a user might simulate investing in a range of cryptocurrencies, tracking how their choices impact digital portfolios over time. What emerges from these experiences is a foundational appreciation for market dynamics that otherwise remain veiled.

Cryptocurrency dramatically shifts financial literacy models, making them more inclusive and accessible than ever before. These tools support policy makers who need to grasp the implications of blockchain and crypto regulation, enabling informed decision-making processes. For aspiring investors and students eager to learn, crypto education becomes a gateway to understanding financial terminologies with ease and context. An individual's path to financial literacy is thereby streamlined as they naturally acquire language and expertise that once seemed daunting.

Practical experiences extend beyond professional spheres, making financial education accessible to all kinds of learners. Crypto rewards systems can make learning financially beneficial. Platforms where learners amass tokens or small crypto amounts as they complete modules, create real incentives for continued education. It's a dynamic shift from traditional learning methods, highlighting the innovative spirit at the heart of crypto culture.

As the chapter continues, the focus shifts to exploring the seamless integration of cryptocurrencies in boosting financial literacy through online courses, crypto-based rewards, and interactive simulations. These initiatives represent a natural progression in modernizing educational landscapes. They underscore the creativity and adaptability needed to stay relevant as financial technologies evolve. Moving forward in our exploration, we delve into how these approaches inspire educators and learners alike, ensuring that financial literacy is not only achievable but an engaging and rewarding pursuit.

Examination of Specific Initiatives Using Cryptocurrencies to Enhance Financial Education

Cryptocurrencies aren't just about investments, risky transactions, or being a tech-savvy trend. As we've previously discussed, their underlying technologies can unravel financial complexities, making room for an era where learning finance can be engaging and practical. Today, we dive into how these digital assets are revolutionizing financial literacy, transforming how individuals worldwide approach this vital life skill, and breaking the chains of traditional finance education.

Let's start by visiting the concept of financial literacy, where fostering an understanding is crucial. Financial literacy is not just about managing money but understanding the dynamics of how financial systems work. Cryptocurrencies have made this learning process active and exciting through numerous initiatives aimed at education. One can't help but notice the emergence of online platforms offering courses tailored to the curious mind thirsty to know how Bitcoin works or the mysteries of Ethereum. Websites like Coursera or platforms with vested interests like Coinbase extend their resources to educate people on using and trading cryptocurrencies through structured courses.

But there's more than just learning from a static screen. Imagine being actively involved through incentive-based learning, which has found a new partner in cryptocurrencies. This incentive model sparks motivation unlike any traditional educational method.

Platforms like BitDegree, for example, reward learners with tokens as they progress through courses specially designed for financial literacy and blockchain technology. This reward system mirrors the gaming industry, compelling learners to engage deeply and unlock new knowledge levels, while learning at their own pace, making education less of a task and more of an adventure.

Every journey through financial learning must include hands-on experience. Enter interactive simulations—this is where fintech meets innovation. Initiatives such as those by Decentraland or CryptoKitties extend beyond passive learning. They immerse users in virtual environments where they actively learn by doing, simulating real-world financial transactions. Through these platforms, learners gain practical experience—buying, selling, or trading digital assets in a risk-free and enjoyable setting. These interactive simulations facilitate a concrete understanding of real-world financial behaviors and trends, offering a sandbox where students can make mistakes without real-life financial repercussions.

Real-life application enhances learning, integrating financial concepts into tangible skills. Initiatives like Binance Academy offer educational resources and tutorials where learners not only engage with theoretical knowledge but absorb practical know-how on trading strategies, the dynamics of the stock market, and blockchain tech. The academy not only promotes the understanding of finance but endeavors to equip its audience with tools required to navigate the cryptocurrency world confidently.

These platforms succeed because they make financial literacy courses intrinsically exciting and valuable. Tracking solid examples, the University of Nicosia in Cyprus stands as a pioneering academic institution offering a Master of Science Degree focusing on Digital Currency. They embed comprehensive coursework that delves into the economic, legal, and technical foundations of cryptocurrencies and blockchain. As a pioneer in adopting blockchain technology, this initiative illustrates how traditional education institutions recognize and adapt to the changing landscape of financial learning.

Cryptocurrency meets charity, as well, when sharing knowledge. Charitable organizations like GiveCrypto not only distribute cryptocurrencies to families in need—they come with an educational program that ensures recipients understand how it works, boosting their financial knowledge alongside their resources. Such initiatives stress the importance of education and financial empowerment as a means to alleviate poverty and build financial resilience, casting a wider educational net that cuts across demographics and economic barriers.

Seen through a global lens, countries like Japan are introducing blockchain technology in their educational curricula, aiming to build a financially literate future generation. Government-supported programs and educational reforms incorporate cryptocurrencies into high school syllabuses, inspiring younger generations to explore how decentralized finance impacts global markets. This impulse towards integrating digital currency education into mainstream education systems globally signifies a burgeoning shift in the fundamental understanding of finance.

These educational forays into cryptocurrencies offer more than immediate financial gains for participants. They prepare learners for upcoming market trends, embedding a deep-seated awareness of global financial networks. Students learn to critique investment strategies, understand risk management, and evaluate the potential impacts of decentralized finance on everyday life. These lessons apply to potential investment opportunities and nurture critical thinking, a trait indispensable for personal financial decision-making.

Anticipating the next evolution, blockchain technology opens doors for educational transparency and credibility. As we are about to delve into, cutting-edge developments are paving the way for blockchain-based credentialing systems, an emerging innovation we'll explore next. These systems promise the ability to provide verifiable educational achievements, easily shareable and trusted across institutions and employers alike. The potential impact here is vast—reducing fraudulent claims and increasing trust within the field of education.

Moreover, open-access resources are profoundly altering the educational landscape. Through blockchain, resource-sharing becomes reliable and more accessible than ever, breaking financial and geographical barriers that previously hindered educational access. This ensures that knowledge reaches underserved communities and individuals who might not have otherwise had the opportunity to benefit from formal financial education.

Financial literacy is no longer confined to textbooks or lecture halls. It's in our digital wallets, our online investments, and increasingly in our everyday interactions. The proliferation of cryptocurrency-based educational initiatives opens new dimensions for learners at all stages of life. By embracing these changes, you gain the tools and insights to navigate a rapidly evolving financial environment, shaping not just your future but the future of financial education itself.

With technological advancements on the horizon, blockchain credentialing and open access are concepts knocking at the door. They promise a seamless transition into a world where your educational journey is transparent, trusted, and unbounded by global barriers. Ready to step into this future with us?

Discussion on Global Efforts Making Education Accessible Worldwide Through Various Technologies

Many of us have already seen how cryptocurrencies and related technologies are redefining the way we understand and interact with financial systems. Online courses and crypto-based educational platforms are at the forefront, enhancing financial literacy by offering practical, real-world simulations. These tools are immersive, allowing users to participate in activities that reinforce financial management concepts without the need for high-stakes environments. With real-time feedback and adaptable difficulty levels, they provide a continuous learning experience that is tailored to individual needs.

As we look deeper, we encounter the broader implications of cryptocurrency becoming an integral part of education worldwide. One prominent benefit is accessibility, achieved through blockchain-based credentialing systems. Such systems break down traditional barriers by decentralizing educational control. Historically, recognized qualifications were often restricted to those within specific socioeconomic brackets. Now, blockchain technology can verify achievements without traditional gatekeepers, ensuring that skills and knowledge are validated and recognized across borders. For example, in developing nations where infrastructure challenges exist, educational access via blockchain credentials can transform lives by making opportunities tangible and actionable.

But the influence doesn't stop at credentialing. Open-access educational resources, made possible through collaborative cryptocurrencies, have sprouted, offering educational materials at little to no cost. Textbooks, lectures, and interactive modules are increasingly available online, sometimes in a decentralized format that eliminates intermediaries altogether. Communities of educators can build and refine course materials that meet current demands, share them openly, and continuously update them to reflect the evolving socio-economic landscapes. This fosters a culture of collaboration where knowledge is highly valued and freely shared, driving down costs and vastly

increasing accessibility.
Consider the internet access innovations powered by cryptocurrency technologies. Projects that employ microloans and community-backed funding mechanisms stand out. By financially enabling infrastructure projects, they extend low-cost or even free internet access to remote communities. This brings the world's educational resources to the fingertips of those who might otherwise remain isolated. Such initiatives mean that a child in a rural setting could potentially access the same quality educational materials as a student in a major city. Equity in education becomes more than an ideal—it becomes a tangible reality.

Each of these elements ties back to the larger picture of financial literacy, bringing diverse demographics into the digital fold. Financial habits, for those unfamiliar with modern banking, are slowly shifting thanks to exposure to crypto-based educational platforms. Understanding and managing digital wallets, engaging with safe trading practices, and making informed investment choices create a cadre of financially literate individuals who are better prepared for the digital economy's fast-paced changes. This shift is crucial as more countries explore digital currencies and the global market becomes increasingly interconnected.
To better understand these advancements' societal impacts, we must assess specific framework examples already in action. Take the case of the Open University, which has employed blockchain technology to issue certificates. Students can complete courses and have their credentials instantly verified both by employers and educational institutions worldwide, bypassing cumbersome traditional verification processes. Another stimulating example is the tie-up between certain blockchain platforms and rural development programs. Here, blockchain's transparent nature ensures that resources reach intended beneficiaries, without diversionary leaks, enhancing educational projects' integrity and credibility.

Moreover, educational platforms driven by cryptocurrencies are enriching learning experiences far beyond basic financial concepts. Look at initiatives that incorporate gamification techniques, offering virtual rewards for learning milestones. This blend of education with incentive-driven activities keeps learners engaged longer and promotes a more profound understanding. Students might work their way through real-world national economic scenarios or global financial crises in a simulated environment, equipping them with practical and strategic thinking skills.
In closing, it's crucial to understand how cryptocurrency and educational frameworks continue to intertwine, creating robust pathways for financial literacy. As technology advances, integrating sophisticated algorithms into learning management systems could further lower educational access barriers. AI-driven personalized learning paths and crypto incentive systems might become standard practice, leading to diverse educational settings' evolution.
As we move forward, the potential for these technologies to empower individuals economically becomes increasingly apparent. They stir up hope for unleashing human potential on a massive scale, democratizing education by granting unprecedented access to resources historically reserved for the few. With financial literacy rising globally, communities are equipped to tap into broader market opportunities, foster entrepreneurship, and drive socio-economic development meaningfully. The world we envision—a world of empowered, financially savvy individuals—is within reach, thanks

to the relentless intersections of crypto and educational innovation.

Conclusion Highlighting the Synergy Between Crypto Advancements and Educational Initiatives for Financial Literacy

As we consider the role of cryptocurrencies in financial education, it's crucial to recognize the foundation set by technological advancements that have revolutionized global access to learning. We've seen how technology broadens educational horizons, transcending geographical and financial barriers. Cryptocurrencies continue this trajectory, making financial literacy more reachable and inclusive. They offer a fresh lens through which education can be transformed, especially in financial contexts where traditional methods often fall short.

Cryptocurrency technologies like blockchain are weaving into educational frameworks, dismantling long-standing hurdles to financial literacy. These digital innovations present economic empowerment opportunities for a wide range of people — from crypto novices dipping their toes into digital currency waters to students eager to dive into modern finance, working professionals seeking continued education, and policymakers striving to understand their implications.

Consider how cryptocurrencies can weave into education modules. Online courses and workshops on platforms such as Coursera and Khan Academy are embedding topics like Bitcoin and blockchain into their curriculum, offering learners straightforward, interactive, and practical knowledge. Engagement in these digital financial aspects makes learning more dynamic and reflective of actual economic environments.

Blockchain-based systems play a significant role in credentialing and securing educational resources. They authenticate qualifications with unparalleled reliability, removing the bureaucratic and often error-prone processes traditional systems entail. Students and institutions benefit from a more credible and accessible educational experience. Through smart contracts, for instance, course completions and degrees become verifiable, reducing fraud and enhancing trust in educational achievements.

Applications of these technologies fuel financial literacy by providing learners with real-world engagements. When individuals can mimic the use of digital assets in a controlled, educational environment, they connect theoretical knowledge with practical usage. For instance, virtual simulations allow students to manage crypto wallets, execute transactions, or even venture into digital asset investment with no risk. These experiences critically enhance their understanding of complex financial systems.

In some communities and educational settings, cryptocurrencies facilitate funding of educational projects. Take the example of decentralized finance platforms offering crypto grants or scholarships, democratizing access to education for many who might otherwise be financially constrained. By reducing traditional funding dependencies, cryptocurrencies ensure a wider reach, sparking increases in financial acumen and understanding across demographics.

Crypto-based initiatives illustrate their potential to raise financial literacy. Imagine a scenario where a school integrates blockchain directly into its curriculum, enabling students to understand digital assets' role by managing school-based tokens. These tokens could represent anything from reward points for academic excellence to engagement metrics in school activities. Such hands-on experience teaches students the nuances of digital transactions and connects theoretical finance with everyday applications.

Moreover, how cryptocurrencies simplify complex financial concepts promotes simplified understanding. An institution might use a simulated blockchain ledger in their teaching strategy. As learners record and analyze transactions, they witness firsthand how value transfers, learn consensus algorithms, and appreciate decentralized systems. This method provides clarity on decentralized finance that textbooks or lectures alone might not achieve.

Crypto technologies drive democratized learning environments. Platforms employing decentralized ledger technologies decentralize power away from traditional banks and financial gatekeepers, thus serving communities usually excluded by traditional finance. As people access these resources, financial literacy grows, offering not just knowledge but a path towards tangible economic participation.

We also see crypto systems fostering transparency. Consider how traditional financial education often hinges on understanding opaque mechanisms of credit scores or interest calculations. In contrast, the transparent nature of blockchain transactions demystifies these practices. Students learn about financial exchanges through clear, public blockchain records, promoting a deeper comprehension of financial pledges and outcomes.

The case studies are numerous. From Finland's implementation of blockchain in academic credentialing to Uganda's crypto scholarships for higher education, the global stage showcases progress. Although these initiatives battle regulatory and infrastructural challenges, their emergence signifies a shift towards inclusive financial education.

Cryptocurrencies also give rise to new financial ecosystems through which individuals can explore decentralized finance possibilities. By engaging with these ecosystems, learners develop insights into an economy functioning outside traditional banking norms. They comprehend the full spectrum of financial literacy — from asset management to risk assessment, broadening their economic expertise.

Overall, cryptocurrency technologies empower a more educated populace through their inherent qualities. From breaking down past financial barriers to providing practical applications and ensuring equity in educational opportunities, their impact is multifaceted. This ongoing transformation in financial education lays a robust groundwork for a diverse and inclusive economic future, making financial literacy a shared asset for all demographics.

Cryptocurrencies and blockchain technologies amplify educational frameworks, tying economic empowerment with accessible learning. From credential authentication to real-world application in educational settings, the transformative power they hold ensures all individuals can participate in a financially literate world. As these technologies advance, they promise to rewrite the book on financial education, continuously inviting more voices into the conversation.

Bringing It All Together

As we navigate the evolving landscape of financial literacy through the lens of cryptocurrencies, it's evident that these digital innovations are reshaping our understanding of money and finance. Cryptocurrencies, with their decentralized nature, offer a unique entry point into grasping complex financial systems, making abstract concepts accessible to newcomers and experts alike. They encourage practical learning by engaging users in real-world applications—whether it's managing a crypto wallet, participating in decentralized finance, or simply transacting digitally. This hands-on approach demystifies previously obscure financial processes, empowering individuals from various walks of life to embrace financial literacy with confidence and curiosity. As we look forward, the potential for cryptocurrencies to further democratize education and financial inclusion is vast. By integrating these technologies into educational frameworks, we can enhance accessibility, enrich learning experiences, and ultimately bridge economic opportunities across diverse populations. This chapter sets the stage for deeper discussions on how leveraging these tools can revolutionize our approach to financial education, ensuring it becomes a universally accessible resource. Now that we understand the transformative power of cryptocurrencies in education, we can explore how these technologies will continue to shape the future of financial literacy on a global scale.

Chapter 11: *Regulation, Risks, and Responsible Use*

The world of cryptocurrency and blockchain is like a new frontier, filled with promise and trepidation. Imagine the exhilaration of discovering uncharted territory, where digital assets are the currency of the future and traditional finance watches from the sidelines. Yet, along with this thrill, there's uncertainty—a landscape where regulations haven't caught up, risks loom large, and responsible use becomes more crucial than ever. Just like the early explorers who ventured into the unknown, today's crypto enthusiasts find themselves navigating a landscape that's both exciting and unpredictable.
Throughout this chapter, we delve into how regulation serves as the crucial channel marker in the turbulent waters of digital commerce, preventing calamitous drift into the dangerous shoals of uncertainty. We also unpack the potential hazards lurking within these waters, emphasizing the significance of informed, responsible navigation. As you journey through these pages, you'll gain insights into how these elements intersect, ultimately creating a balanced and secure environment that supports innovation without compromising safety.

Introducing Regulation, Risks, and Responsible Use
Navigating the world of cryptocurrency and blockchain feels like stepping into a new frontier, one that's both exciting and fraught with risks. Regulation plays a huge role here. It acts as the guardrails that keep technology on track. Without it, the risks could become overwhelming, both for individual investors and the broader financial system. Take, for example, the chaos when regulations fail to keep up with rapid technological advancements. The collapse of certain crypto exchanges, where user funds evaporated into the digital ether due to lack of oversight, serves as a cautionary tale of what happens when structures meant to protect us lag behind.
This is where the relationship between regulation, risk management, and responsible use takes center stage. Regulation exists not to stifle innovation but to ensure it results in fair, stable, and secure markets. By laying down a legal framework, regulation defines boundaries within which enterprises can safely operate. It separates promising ventures from Ponzi schemes and enhances investor confidence. This, in turn, encourages more participation from traditional finance players, ushering in a wave of capital and legitimacy to the digital assets space. However, merely having rules isn't enough; strict enforcement and timely updates to these regulations often determine their effectiveness.

Let's consider a real-world instance where lack of regulation led to chaos. A few years ago, an anonymous developer launched a cryptocurrency with promises of astronomical returns. Many new investors, swayed by the potential for fast profits, poured money into it without understanding its mechanics. The currency surged in value, driven by speculation, but eventually collapsed. The aftermath left many personal fortunes shattered, highlighting that while high returns tempt, they often come with high risks. Regulatory bodies then swooped in, but it was too late for those caught in the frenzy.
On the flip side, when we look at scenarios with robust regulation, the picture is

different. Regulatory measures can take various forms, from strict compliance requirements to regular audits. These measures create a reliable environment where responsible use can flourish. Responsible use involves informed decisions by individuals and institutions, promoting behaviors that mitigate excessive risk-taking. This means staying informed, understanding the terms and conditions of any crypto investment, and acknowledging the often-volatile nature of digital currencies. For instance, funds legally bound to report their crypto holdings offer transparency and reassurance to their investors. The result is a market less prone to sudden crashes and scandals, where the focus shifts toward utilizing blockchain technology for genuine advancement—whether through decentralized applications, security advancements, or even promoting societal good.

Of course, the juxtaposition of regulation and liberty is a sensitive one. Many view cryptocurrency as a way to escape oppressive traditional banking systems. This ideal of decentralization, and the freedom it supposedly brings, attracts those wary of governmental oversight. Yet, unchecked freedom often leads to exploitation. For instance, Initial Coin Offerings (ICOs) emerged as a way to fund blockchain-based projects but quickly became breeding grounds for scams when the hype overshadowed due diligence. Regulation becomes vital in ensuring decentralized systems don't devolve into chaotic free-for-alls but rather evolve into systems that benefit everyone. Furthermore, regulation acts as a guidepost for technological ethics as blockchain's potential stretches beyond finance. Consider digital identity systems built on the blockchain, which promise better security and privacy. Here, regulation is crucial to ensure data is handled responsibly. By embedding ethical considerations into the core of emerging technologies, regulators can safeguard against the misuse of data and promote applications that benefit society as a whole, such as secure voting systems or fairer credit scoring.

Transitioning into a responsible crypto market also requires a well-informed populace. Education plays a crucial role here. Users, whether newbies or seasoned investors, must understand how regulatory frameworks impact their interactions with digital currency. Simple decisions, like choosing a wallet provider or participating in a blockchain project, hinge on knowing the regulatory landscape. Informed users make choices that align with their risk tolerance and ethical standards. Regulatory bodies, alongside private and public institutions, must invest in awareness programs—ensuring that everyone, from students to policymakers, is equipped to navigate and shape this new world.

As we dive deeper into this realm, the role of regulators should evolve from mere gatekeeping to facilitating dialogue. Given the rapid pace of technological advancements, regulators often find themselves in reactive stances. Bridging this gap requires collaborative efforts between tech innovators, policymakers, and financiers to draft adaptive, forward-thinking regulations. Listening to diverse voices can shed light on unforeseen challenges and opportunities, leading to a robust system that aligns with the underlying ethos of both protection and innovation.

In conclusion, regulation, risk, and the responsible use of cryptocurrency and blockchain technologies form a dynamic triad that anchors the financial ecosystem. Understanding how these elements interact is essential to navigating this exciting digital landscape. As we prepare to explore the critical intricacies of legal frameworks in our next section, remember this interconnectedness. Regulatory clarity and effective governance pave the way for responsible practices that help prevent the pitfalls of previous financial booms and busts. With these principles in mind, the crypto and blockchain domain carries the promise of a more inclusive and secure financial future for everyone.

Navigating Legal Landscapes

The intersection of regulation, risks, and responsible use becomes vital as cryptocurrency weaves itself into our financial and technological landscapes. Understanding these interconnected elements strengthens the foundation of our forays into this brave, new world. Regulation does not aim to stifle innovation but to create a safe environment where advancements can flourish. As such, grasping the importance of legal frameworks guides us toward responsible crypto adoption.

In delving into the importance of understanding legal frameworks, we must first acknowledge the varied landscape of global regulatory environments. Different regions approach cryptocurrency with varying levels of acceptance and skepticism. For instance, the European Union offers a relatively progressive stance, aiming for harmonized regulation across member states through initiatives like the Markets in Crypto-Assets (MiCA) regulation. By contrast, regions such as China have taken a more restrictive approach, banning certain activities outright. The United States presents a patchwork of regulations, with federal oversight complemented by individual state policies. These disparities stress the need for thorough comprehension of these frameworks to navigate the global market responsibly.

Recognizing how regulations impact individual users, businesses, and investors helps demystify the sometimes-intimidating facade of legal requirements. For an individual user, understanding regulations means more than avoiding scams; it involves knowing the rights and protections in place, such as anti-money laundering (AML) measures and know-your-customer (KYC) protocols. Such regulations ensure that individuals participate within a framework that prizes security. Consider an investor looking to enter the crypto market; compliance with securities laws and tax obligations not only avoids punitive measures but also bolsters investor confidence. For businesses operating in the blockchain space, adherence to regulations ensures legitimacy and trust, both from a customer standpoint and in the eyes of potential partners. Coinbase, for instance, has consistently highlighted its compliance with regulations as a selling point for its services—this approach underscores its commitment to responsible business practices.

The evolution of cryptocurrency regulations has traveled a winding road from the inception of Bitcoin to today. Initially viewed as an unregulated haven, the crypto space faced criticisms for enabling illicit activities and fostering instability. However, mounting adoption forced regulators to adapt. For example, the Financial Action Task Force (FATF) introduced guidelines to combat money laundering and terrorism financing involving virtual assets. Such adaptations show a dynamic interplay between regulatory bodies and the rapid proliferation of blockchain technologies. Furthermore, regulators today are contemplating a future where emerging topics like decentralized finance (DeFi) and non-fungible tokens (NFTs) require novel regulatory approaches. Thus, understanding current legal frameworks prepares us to anticipate and adapt to these future shifts.

Real-world scenarios illustrate these points vividly. Consider the case of cryptocurrency exchanges. They often fall within regulatory purviews that demand registration with

financial authorities and compliance with AML and KYC requirements. Failure to adhere can result in significant fines or business cessation. BitMEX, a prominent exchange, faced legal action in the United States for violating AML laws—this incident serves as a reminder of the biting consequences of neglecting regulatory frameworks. On the positive side, exchanges and projects complying with regulations often see increased trust from users, as it provides a sense of security against fraudulent activities.
This brings us to the role regulations play in safeguarding against legal and financial pitfalls. The legal frameworks around cryptocurrency not only protect against fraud but also offer clarity amidst market volatility. In an ever-evolving landscape, adherence to these frameworks assures stability. Regulatory compliance can deter hasty or uninformed decisions that typically precede significant crypto losses. For instance, the requirement of proper market conduct rules keeps players on even footing, reducing the risk of market manipulation and ensuring fair competition.

With regulations providing such a critical foundation, understanding them emerges as a valuable asset in risk management strategies. Being conversant with these rules equips participants with the tools needed to navigate complexities confidently. As cryptocurrencies evolve and new functionalities emerge, such as smart contracts and decentralized apps, regulatory scrutiny will likely increase. The informed participants will be the ones who can quickly adapt, seize opportunities, and proceed with integrity. Navigating the crypto world without this comprehension becomes akin to sailing blind. You would miss the opportunity to mitigate liabilities or adapt to change, potentially tarnishing reputations or inviting undue legal scrutiny. Thus, cultivating a robust understanding of the regulations enables participants to engage with the sector responsibly.
As we contemplate future trajectories, regulations will likely grow more intricate and globally coordinated. The potential for international cybercrime, alongside rising investment stakes, ensures that regulatory bodies will continually seek robust measures. In anticipation, a proactive approach to understanding these frameworks bodes well. Those well-versed in this regulatory interplay will find themselves better positioned to weather shifts, adapt to novel requirements, and steer clear of legal quagmires.

This section sets a foundation for tackling the intricate lies and truths within the space. Regulatory knowledge stands as the first line of defense against fraudulent activities, equipping you to discern authentic operations from deceitful ones. As we look to exploring the ways to identify and steer clear of scams, recall the value of regulations in this endeavor. It's this knowledge that positions you—be you a user, an investor, or a business owner—to partake actively and responsibly in this revolutionary space.

Understanding Scams in Risk Contexts

Understanding legal requirements creates a foundation, but it's only part of the puzzle when adopting responsible practices in the cryptocurrency world. Recognizing scams demands equal attention to shield against potential pitfalls. Many find the crypto landscape enticing because of its innovative appeal and opportunities for growth. However, this allure also draws in nefarious actors who seek to exploit hopeful investors. Scams thrive in this space due to its relative novelty, anonymity, and decentralization, making it imperative to recognize common threats.
Phishing remains a prevalent trap. Scammers often disguise themselves as reputable

companies through emails, social media, or fake websites to capture private keys or personal information. An apparent giveaway could be misleading URLs or demanding urgent action, prompting haste over verification. Knowing this, always verify the source by checking official communication channels. Additionally, secure communication practices, such as using two-factor authentication, reduce phishing risks.

Ponzi schemes, wherein returns for older investors are funded by the contributions of newer ones, pose another threat. Promises of guaranteed high returns with little risk scream caution. Legitimate investments never offer such assurances. Be skeptical of schemes that lack transparency about how they generate returns. Always demand clear, logical explanations of investment strategies. If these seem purposely vague, question them further. Remember, if it sounds too good to be true, it probably is.

Initial Coin Offerings (ICOs) present another complex landscape. While many ICOs have legitimate goals, some take advantage of investors' lack of understanding. Scammers might promote ICOs with glamorous websites and unrealistic roadmaps without credible teams or clear articulation of project viability. To discern legitimate ICOs from scams, research the development team's credentials and past projects. Also, scrutinize whitepapers for detail on innovation's applicability. Comprehensive documents signal transparency, dedication, and doable plans.

By exploring scams, we can see how they're often rooted in manipulating emotions—fear of missing out, greed, or urgency. A firm grasp of human psychology becomes critical alongside financial literacy in recognizing red flags. It's crucial to cultivate a balanced perspective, so we don't fall victim to these emotional traps. This balance ties into recognizing and respecting risk analysis fundamentals. As potential investors or enthusiasts in emerging markets, a comprehensive understanding of these dynamics informs better decisions.

Staying informed about the latest developments across legitimate platforms serves as a shield against scams. Industry reports, vetted crypto news sites, and forums such as GitHub or Reddit provide insights and community perspectives. Engaging in community discussions fosters collective vigilance against scams. These forums act as a watchdog where shared experiences and insights create an informed user base. Also, security measures safeguard assets. Using robust and unique passwords, enabling two-factor authentication, and employing hardware wallets enhance security layers.

It's important to understand how recognizing scams is fundamental to managing broader risks. Without this knowledge, the foundation of risk management strategies might falter, impacting decision-making processes. Once knowledgeable about these scams, we can better assess market volatility, a hallmark of cryptocurrency investment risk. Clear understanding allows recognition of price swings not merely as threats but as potential opportunities by adopting learned risk management strategies.

Market volatility stems from factors like regulatory announcements, technological advancements, or broader economic shifts. Grasping these fluctuations becomes less daunting when assessing them through the lens of informed risk assessment.

Recognizing the effects of scams on volatility accentuates the need for transparency and reliability within the market. It positions informed investors not just to react but to strategize effectively, recognizing investment's innate uncertainty.

The narrative of scams, tightly interwoven with risk management, forms a cornerstone for those venturing into cryptocurrency. It bolsters resilience against potential losses by embracing risk's dual nature—danger and opportunity. At the heart of responsible use lies comprehension of both individual actions' implications and larger market forces. Through this dual awareness, we harness cryptocurrency's potential rather than fall prey to its pitfalls.

By acknowledging the potential for scams, newcomers are better equipped to handle the acute challenges of market volatility and risk management. Being forewarned helps in creating robust strategies vital for thriving in such rapidly evolving domains. Recognizing scams empowers aspirants to navigate the stormy seas of cryptocurrency with securely anchored boats.

Therefore, as we delve deeper into cryptocurrency-related discussions, let's carry forward this integrated insight of scams and risk management into understanding market volatility. It's not merely about keeping assets safe—it's about nurturing a mindset that comprehends and embraces risk wisely and responsibly. This informed stance shapes a future where cryptocurrency becomes a sphere not of fear but of calculated opportunity—always alert, always ready.

Embarking on this learning journey, recognizing scams as a foundational element of risk management, we seamlessly segue into broader conversations about market volatility and its implications for sound decision-making processes. Understanding how they interconnect forms a base from which informed discussions continue into the intricacies of market dynamics and their influence on strategic financial choices. Through this progression, the dialogue remains informed, engaging, and above all, unwaveringly rooted in responsible practices.

Market Volatility Considerations

Previously, we navigated the murky waters of cryptocurrency scams, learning to recognize and avoid the pitfalls that scammers set. This foundation isn't just about spotting Red Flags but primes our understanding of market volatility, a key player in the broader landscape of risks. It's essential to comprehend how an awareness of scams may inadvertently sharpen our instincts regarding other market threats, like instability. When you know where scams lurk, you inherently become more attuned to other forms of risk, especially those born from sudden and drastic market shifts.

Market volatility may often be perceived as the heartbeat of cryptocurrency, with dramatic highs and stomach-churning lows. These fluctuations result from a myriad of factors: trading volumes, large-scale market activities, or even global events. For seasoned investors, these swings aren't just ripples to navigate but rather waves that dictate the course of their risk management strategies. Novices in this field might wonder how such volatility could shape investment decisions, but to professionals, it's clear: each peak and trough demands meticulous thought and potentially significant changes to one's strategy.

Picture the market as a dynamic playfield where yesterday's move could swiftly become tomorrow's regret. Volatile markets invite not just adventures in opportunity but a dance with danger. Recognizing these risks is not just about predicting patterns but also understanding how these shifts can amplify cybersecurity threats. For instance, when markets swing wildly, scammers become more active, looking for cracks in reputations, which might appear due to fear and uncertainty. The interplay between market volatility and the threat landscape requires a holistic approach to risk evaluation.

Let's take a closer look at how market volatility has previously and profoundly impacted strategic decision-making. One of the most striking examples is the cryptocurrency crash of 2018. During this period, Bitcoin lost a significant chunk of its value, along with other cryptocurrencies. Investors, who once thought their holdings were ironclad, had to pivot swiftly, adjusting their strategies to mitigate losses. Some diversified their portfolios, spreading the risk across different assets, while others sought refuge in stablecoins.

Such historical lessons are invaluable, but even hypothetical scenarios can be enlightening. Imagine a new regulatory announcement causing uncertainty in the market. This news could prompt investors to hedge their bets, sell off risky assets, or hold onto their investments in hopes of future recoveries. Illustrating these scenarios helps newcomers grasp the nuances of decision-making in tumultuous markets and prepares them for real-world challenges.

Education in risk management cannot stop at simply reacting to market shifts. Instead, it promotes understanding that each movement entails a spider-web of consequences stretching from immediate financial impacts to broader cybersecurity concerns. Hence, fostering a defensive mindset means continuously evaluating risks against reward, reassessing portfolios, and ensuring digital safety measures are intact.

Navigating this landscape involves more than just individual vigilance. Networking with other market participants can provide insights, invaluable advice, and validation for risky decisions. Community engagement is crucial in an environment where information changes rapidly, and insights can mean the difference between a hard fall and a graceful retreat.

Ensuring clarity, while maintaining a conversational and authoritative voice, lets us demystify these complex topics for newcomers. The goal is to make these considerations intuitive, arming you with not just the knowledge but the confidence to act swiftly and effectively. When volatility rears its unpredictable head, knowing when to hold, adjust or fold isn't just strategic but essential to survival.

We should be mindful of not just the pitfalls of redundancy but the clarity of new perspectives. Each point in this discussion should build upon the last, deepening your understanding and furnishing you with a toolkit of strategies and considerations. We aim not to repeat, but to layer, to construct a meaningful dialogue that draws you deeper into the field.

As this section concludes, prepare to transition seamlessly into a more solution-oriented conversation. Next, we will delve into practical strategies and best practices designed to enhance safety and mitigate risks across the sprawling challenges of cryptocurrency engagement. By weaving an understanding of volatility into a tapestry of actionable insights, you step forward equipped to not only face uncertainties head-on but to thrive within them. With clarity and foresight, the next section promises to arm you with the necessary tools and knowledge.

Strategies for Staying Safe

In our journey through the crypto landscape, we've tackled the whirlwind of market volatility. This volatility doesn't just influence pricing; it reverberates through risk management strategies and decision-making. Understanding how to navigate these choppy waters sets a solid foundation for implementing strategies that prioritize safety and risk mitigation.

First, let's consider the necessity for robust security protocols. Think of these as your first line of defense. After all, the decentralized nature of cryptocurrencies makes them inherently attractive to hackers. Implementing two-factor authentication (2FA) provides a straightforward yet powerful barrier against unauthorized access. This method extends security beyond mere passwords, requiring something you know (your password) and something you have (like a phone) for entry.

Consider cold storage for significant holdings as well. Offline storage isn't vulnerable to online breaches, making it a safe choice for long-term investors. For those actively trading or using their crypto regularly, hardware wallets provide a tangible, secure way to manage your digital assets.

Updating software regularly ensures you take advantage of the latest security patches. Cryptocurrencies run on complex systems, and updates frequently address vulnerabilities. Embracing a proactive attitude towards software updates is crucial—think of it as keeping the doors to your house locked and the alarm system well-maintained.

Beyond individual practices, the community plays a role in security. Participating in communities, forums, and social media platforms can help you stay informed of threats and updates to industry best practices. Being actively engaged with the experiences of others adds an educational layer, reinforcing your knowledge base and resilience against potential pitfalls.

Regulatory awareness is another key pillar. Many countries require compliance with anti-money laundering (AML) and know your customer (KYC) protocols. These regulations aren't just bureaucratic hurdles; they directly impact the safety and legitimacy of platforms. Engaging with exchanges complying with these standards reduces risk and reflects a commitment to transparency and responsibility.

In light of regulations, another helpful strategy is diversifying crypto holdings. By spreading your investment across various projects and tokens, you minimize the risk associated with any single asset's volatility. Diversification helps buffer against market dips and shifts, providing a more balanced, resilient portfolio.

Education plays a crucial role in understanding and managing the unique circumstances of the crypto world. Continuous learning allows you to adapt to technological and strategic changes. Dive into white papers, follow reputable crypto news outlets, and engage with educational resources to stay informed. Knowledge is the bridge between awareness and action, providing the tools necessary to navigate safely through the crypto terrain.

Considering volatile markets discussed earlier, market-specific strategies are indispensable. Using stop-loss orders can effectively prevent significant losses. By setting a price limit at which an asset is sold, you maintain control over your holdings and mitigate any unexpected downtrends. This proactive strategy aligns with your established risk tolerance, ensuring you don't fall victim to emotional decision-making in fast-moving markets.

Moreover, limit orders specify conditions under which transactions execute, offering a structured approach to buying and selling. Limit orders allow you to anticipate market fluctuations and strategically set parameters for your trades, anchoring decision-making with rationality and discipline.

Security ultimately intertwines with knowledge of digital forensic protection, which focuses on identifying and managing suspicious activities across platforms. Engaging with forensic analytic services helps pinpoint unusual activities and issue real-time alerts. These services often work in tandem with exchanges, providing an added layer of defense against sophisticated threats.

To illustrate these strategies, consider a financial advisor's portfolio approach. Diversifying between traditional and digital assets reduces risk exposure while maximizing growth opportunities. Similarly, applying this diversified strategy in the crypto sphere, you spread risk across different investment vehicles, lessening the shock from potential cryptocurrency-specific downturns.

Another clear example comes from using automated bots to execute trades based on predetermined criteria. These bots, tailored with specific strategy algorithms, eliminate emotional trading, carrying out transactions with precision and discipline, which aids significantly during volatile market times.

Ensuring security and reducing risks also extend to operational habits. Avoid sharing private key information through insecure channels. Social engineering and phishing scams often succeed by exploiting human tendencies toward familiarity and complacency. Employing a zero-trust philosophy guards sensitive data, encouraging strict scrutiny of all sharing avenues.

Establishing a "crypto routine" helps maintain an organized approach. Document all transactions carefully, keep track of wallet addresses, and systematically file documents related to your holdings. This practice provides an audit trail and helps manage your portfolio efficiently.

Data protection institutions recommend backing up wallet information using reputable cloud services or encrypted storage devices. This ensures you retain access to your wallet and funds even in unforeseen events like device failures.

When engaging with exchanges or platforms, choose those prioritizing user education and security transparency. Assessing the platform's history, user reviews, and regulatory compliance levels offers insight into their reliability and security commitment. Platforms that clearly communicate security practices and include educational resources generally indicate a mature, user-focused approach.

Lastly, the social fabric of the crypto community can't be ignored. Engage with it wisely. Contributing to forums and discussion groups enhances collective intelligence and supports environment-wide security measures. By exchanging experiences, you reinforce knowledge across the community, promoting safer practices for everyone involved.

In the evolving crypto realm, security involves a compulsive attention to detail across technological, behavioral, and community levels. Implement these versatile strategies as building blocks for a secure, responsible crypto experience. As you explore further into the digital currency universe, you'll encounter diverse challenges but also abundant opportunities for growth and innovation.

Concluding Thoughts

As we wrap up our exploration of regulation, risks, and responsible use in the fast-paced world of cryptocurrency and blockchain, it's clear that understanding these elements is crucial to navigating this exciting yet challenging digital landscape. Regulation acts as a guiding force, balancing innovation with safety, while risk management helps protect both individual investors and the broader financial ecosystem. By fostering responsible use, participants can make informed decisions, reducing excessive risks and enhancing market stability. Now that we know this, we are better prepared to explore the complexities of legal frameworks and their role in shaping a more secure and inclusive financial future. Embracing regulatory clarity and effective governance will prevent past financial pitfalls and pave the way for a thriving crypto and blockchain domain.

REGULATION, RISKS, AND RESPONSIBLE USE
ADDRESSING KEY CONCERNS
REGULATORY FRAMEWORKS
Governments are developing regulations to protect consumers and ensure market integrity
MITIGATING RISKS
Addressing issues like volatility, fraud, and cybersecurity threats in the crypto space
PROMOTING EDUCATION
Emphasizing responsible use and informed decision-making among users

Chapter 12: *The Future of Money and Society*

The Future of Money and Society
Imagine a world where your morning coffee comes with a side of digital convenience, paid directly from an app that transfers funds seamlessly from your central bank. No middlemen, no waiting for transactions to clear, and certainly no hidden fees. While this might sound like a scene from a futuristic movie, it's closer to reality than you might think. As governments explore the transformative possibilities of Central Bank Digital Currencies (CBDCs), everyday exchanges could become quicker and more accessible. However, this rapid evolution in financial technology prompts essential questions: How will this shift impact traditional banks? What about those currently unbanked or located in remote areas? And most critically, how do we balance privacy concerns with the transparency that digital currencies offer?

As we delve into the future of money and society, we'll explore how CBDCs might redefine economic models and enhance financial inclusion. We will also touch on how these digital advancements intersect with innovative concepts like Universal Basic Income (UBI). By examining these developments, we'll consider not just how they promise to reshape monetary policy, but also how they might transform our daily lives in unexpected ways, challenging conventional notions of currency and economy.
Introduction to Central Bank Digital Currencies (CBDCs)
Central Bank Digital Currencies (CBDCs) are gaining quite a bit of attention these days. Imagine them as digital versions of cash that you could hold in your wallet, except this wallet is more likely on your smartphone or computer. With CBDCs, central banks aim to simplify how we handle money by cutting out the middleman, like banks, as much as possible. Think about everyday transactions—purchasing your morning coffee or transferring money to a family member—being handled directly between you and the central bank. This process could simplify transactions and reduce fees associated with traditional banking.

Even more enticing is the speed at which transactions could occur with CBDCs. Think of sending money abroad or paying an international vendor. Typically, these transactions can be slow and costly due to multiple intermediaries. Digital currencies promise quicker settlements, cutting down on waiting time and fees. This speed not only benefits widespread consumer adoption but also makes it easier for businesses to manage cross-border dealings.
Security is another critical feature of CBDCs. With fewer agents managing the money flow, there's theoretically less room for fraud and error. Furthermore, the transparency of the digital ledger could help combat financial crime by making it harder for illicit activities to go unnoticed. Enhanced traceability of transactions could act as a deterrent to illegal activities, increasing overall trust in the financial system.
Now, where CBDCs could truly shine is in revolutionizing monetary policy. Central banks can take charge in ways unimaginable before. Imagine a world where interest rates are finely tuned through precise, targeted interventions directly reaching the public. By adjusting the supply of money more accurately, central banks can respond to economic changes swiftly and effectively. This could help stabilize economies more efficiently.

With CBDCs, financial inclusion becomes more feasible. Imagine accessing financial services via your smartphone, particularly if you're in a remote area or don't have a bank nearby. By offering a direct line to a central banking system through digital currencies, those without traditional banking services get unprecedented access. This leap can bridge economic divides and enable millions to join the financial ecosystem. One might ask, how would traditional banks handle this shift? Well, they'd face significant challenges. With fewer people needing a conventional bank account, banks could see revenue declines. They'd need to pivot, perhaps offering more value-added services that don't compete directly with CBDCs. This adjustment would require both innovation and resilience from the banking sector.

Challenges extend to regulatory hurdles too. How do we ensure these digital currencies comply with existing financial rules? Establishing a robust regulatory framework will be crucial to managing risks related to cybersecurity threats and ensuring customer privacy.

CBDCs also offer opportunities to revamp existent financial systems. A notable area is cross-border payments, which can be cumbersome today due to different currencies, intermediaries, and regulatory environments. With a unified digital system, cross-border exchanges could become as seamless as local transactions. This can greatly benefit expatriates sending money home, businesses engaged in international trade, or travelers managing finances abroad.

Moreover, the feature of programmability in CBDCs can open up new possibilities. Envision a system where financial aid or welfare can be efficiently distributed with conditions embedded directly into the currency—ensuring funds are spent as intended, such as on healthcare or education, providing policymakers with tools to better target social welfare.

But what about privacy? This digital sphere raises legitimate concerns about how much the government or banks monitor financial activities. It's crucial to balance these concerns with the transparency required to keep the system secure and efficient. Finding this balance will be key to gaining public trust.

Another point of interest is how CBDCs could support combating fraud. By using advanced technologies like blockchain, transactions can be registered immutably, providing a clear, unchangeable record that's difficult to alter. This transparency can protect users by reducing many forms of malicious activity.

Switching focus, it's essential to consider how central banks are already experimenting and testing these CBDC waters cautiously, observing how people and businesses interact with these new forms of money. These pilot programs will uncover potential roadblocks and help refine digital currency systems before widespread adoption.

As we transition to discussing the broader implications of CBDCs, it's clear how their introduction can dismantle traditional banking models and offer innovative solutions to monetary policies. With CBDCs, central banks might craft more flexible, intuitive systems that are more aligned with the needs of an increasingly digital world.

Without existing banks driving financial services, for instance, we could witness new entities entering the financial market, incorporating technology companies or even new types of financial enterprises that capitalize on CBDCs' potential to offer novel services. This evolution could lead to a diversified and dynamic financial landscape.

With this in mind, understanding CBDCs not only expands our view of what's possible in financial interactions but also helps us anticipate how these changes could pave the way for developing more streamlined solutions and environmental-friendly approaches to monetary systems. The future of money and how we interact with it continuously evolves, displaying the potential to create a more inclusive, efficient society, all while maintaining security and flexibility. CBDCs stand to be a vital cog—or perhaps the blueprint—in this evolving machine of our financial future.

Implications of CBDCs on Financial Systems

Previously, we explored how Central Bank Digital Currencies (CBDCs) promise to transform how financial transactions work. Acting as a digital form of central bank money, they ensure secure and efficient transactions, potentially challenging traditional banking operations. Let's dive into the ways CBDCs might impact our financial systems more deeply.

CBDCs have the potential to streamline monetary policies significantly. By offering a more direct channel from central banks to citizens, they can reduce the need for multiple intermediary financial institutions. This directness could simplify monetary policy implementation. Central banks might exert finer control over money supply, adjustments to interest rates could reflect more rapidly, and stimulus payments could reach individuals almost instantly. Imagine a future where the central bank needs to enact monetary policy quickly. By adjusting the interest rates on CBDC holdings, they could influence spending behavior more directly. Such a system contrasts with today's methods that rely heavily on commercial bank cooperation to circulate capital.

While this sounds like an efficient process, it's essential to address the challenges CBDCs may pose to conventional banking. Traditional banks often participate in a complex web of activities, acting as intermediaries in payments, loans, and deposits. The introduction of CBDCs might bypass these roles, particularly when it comes to payments. Consequently, banks may face disruptions to some of their fundamental operations. For instance, if customers prefer holding CBDCs over traditional deposits, banks will need to rethink how they attract deposits and manage liquidity. This scenario demands banks evolve, possibly narrowing their focus to specialized services or exploring innovative financial products to remain relevant.

Such institutional shifts also bring about a need to reexamine risk management strategies within banks. With CBDCs, the classic mechanisms that banking institutions rely on might not be as impactful. This calls for a redefinition of risk assessment frameworks. In the new digital currency landscape, the role of banks might pivot towards providing more niche advisory services, specialized in CBDC management and integration with existing financial portfolios. Imagine walking into a bank in the future, not merely as a place to deposit and withdraw cash but as a hub for strategic financial advice focused on maximizing the utility of your digital currencies.

Moreover, CBDCs may encourage more transparent and efficient payment systems. By design, CBDCs enable real-time tracking and settlement of transactions, which can lead to improved transparency in financial dealings. This characteristic could play a significant role in combating corruption and fraud. For example, governments could track public funds with greater precision, ensuring that money allocated for social programs reaches its intended destination without bureaucratic leakage. Transparent transactions facilitated by CBDCs could help restore trust in financial systems, fostering a sense of security among users.

Nonetheless, these opportunities do not come without challenges. The broader availability of CBDCs raises significant concerns around cybersecurity and privacy. As digital currencies become more widespread, they could become attractive targets for cyber-attacks. Ensuring robust security measures will become paramount in the design and operation of CBDCs. Privacy, too, is a sensitive issue. While transparency can combat illicit activities, it also presents a dilemma for individuals who value financial anonymity. Finding the right balance between transparency and privacy will be crucial. Developers and policymakers need to work together to construct a framework that protects individual rights while maintaining necessary oversight.

Looking at potential changes, CBDCs can alter international trade dynamics. Currently, cross-border transactions often suffer from delays and high fees, mainly due to the multiple financial entities involved. CBDCs could streamline these processes, making international payments faster and cheaper. Imagine emigrant workers able to send money back home with reduced costs, or businesses settling invoices with overseas suppliers in real time. The ripple effect extends to global trade patterns, with nations adopting more seamless integration of financial systems. However, such efficiency might demand stronger international regulations to prevent misuse of these currencies for illegal purposes.

One interesting pathway CBDCs open is the discussion of universal basic income (UBI) distributed digitally. With the capacity to directly issue digital currency to citizens, central banks could support UBI schemes more efficiently and transparently. This could be a powerful tool in battling inequality, offering a safety net that ensures everyone has access to essential resources. But it's not without its challenges, such as determining the source of funding for such schemes and ensuring they don't lead to inflation.

As we transition to the next section, CBDCs hold the potential to reshape monetary policy development fundamentally. Their agility allows central banks to test and refine policy responses in real-time, aligning more closely with economic shifts. Improved transaction transparency emerges as a double-edged sword, presenting an opportunity to enhance trust but also a risk in safeguarding personal privacy. Cybersecurity concerns loom large, demanding that central banks bolster their defense mechanisms to protect against potential threats rigorously.

These discussions are vital as CBDCs move from concept to reality. The choices made in their design and implementation will have far-reaching consequences, not just for financial systems but for how societies function and prosper. As technology and policy continue to evolve, staying informed and engaged is crucial for everyone involved, from policymakers and institutions to individual citizens preparing for this new financial frontier.

The Role of CBDCs in Shaping Future Monetary Policies

In the previous section, we explored the emerging world of central bank digital currencies (CBDCs) and their potential to disrupt traditional financial systems. These digital currencies not only challenge banking operations but also create unique opportunities and hurdles. One key opportunity comes in the form of improved transaction transparency. By nature, digital currencies are far more traceable than cash, and this transparency can help combat illicit financial activities like money laundering or tax evasion. It allows central banks to institute more refined monetary policies with clear insights into economic flows. Yet, with transparency comes the concern of privacy and cybersecurity. As financial transactions become more visible, individuals and organizations alike might fear for their sensitive financial data being exposed or mishandled. This risk necessitates robust cybersecurity measures and thoughtful policymaking aimed at safeguarding privacy while ensuring the smooth functioning of digital currencies.

Take China, for example, a frontrunner in the CBDC race with its digital yuan. Initial results from pilot programs in cities like Shenzhen have been promising, demonstrating increased transaction speed and reduced costs. The government has been able to monitor transaction flows in real-time, providing a very granular view of how money moves across the economy. Similarly, countries like Sweden, with its e-krona, gives us another glimpse into how efficiently a CBDC can integrate with existing systems, potentially decreasing reliance on cash and enhancing the overall monetary framework.

Comparatively, traditional currencies predominantly rely on a complex machine of banking institutions to maintain records and conduct transactions. With CBDCs, the central banks themselves can track and regulate monetary policies directly. This difference considerably elevates the role of central banks in policy-making and implementation. As economies experiment with CBDCs, initial reports suggest an evolving landscape where policymakers can adapt more swiftly to economic shifts, respond better to crises, and experiment with monetary theory applications that were previously impractical with slower-moving money.

While there are undeniable benefits, it's crucial to understand the unique challenges they pose as well. Cyber threats loom as a persistent problem in the digital sphere. Even with robust systems in place, there's always the risk of cyberattacks on the centralized infrastructure that back CBDCs. This can have more immediate and widespread consequences than traditionally seen in decentralized systems. Developing technologies like quantum computing might either pose new threats or possibly provide solutions by creating encryption methods that are currently inconceivable. Policies must evolve alongside these technologies to ensure they are safe and that public trust in the digital money system is maintained.

Another critical component involves how different countries approach the integration of CBDCs, as no one-size-fits-all model exists. China and Sweden have navigated this space with diverse strategies, taking into account distinct privacy norms, political structures, and economic contexts. Through trial and often error, central banks are finding the right balance between transparency and privacy, with some nations choosing more open models, while others might prefer walled-garden approaches.

Yet, even if risks are mitigated, challenges remain in the form of public acceptance and technological literacy. According to sociotechnical models, the success of technological innovation largely depends on public uptake and adaptability. Educating people on CBDC usage, advantages, and security practices becomes a part of monetary policy development, building a digital financial infrastructure that works for everyone.

It's natural to wonder about the broader implications when these issues are ironed out. Here, the potential for CBDCs to stabilize economies points to new financial models like universal basic income (UBI). The controlled environment of CBDCs allows for efficient disbursement and monitoring of UBI payments, reducing administrative costs and ensuring funds reach intended recipients without leakage. This capability, combined with the finer control that digital currencies offer, means central banks could better respond to economic downturns or shocks in a manner that's precise and timely, offering a safety net against both global and localized financial instability.

Some proponents argue that the implementation of UBI could tackle pressing issues, like poverty and income inequality, leveraging the efficiencies introduced by CBDCs. In theory, CBDCs offer a more cost-effective and equitable distribution model than current cash-transfer systems that often suffer due to bureaucratic inefficiencies or corruption. With the backbone of CBDCs, UBI could foster a more secure and guaranteed income level, providing a financial cushion for citizens and encouraging labor market experimentation and flexibility.

As we transition from understanding CBDCs to contemplating the impact of UBI, consider how CBDCs lay a technological foundation. They not only improve the systemic stability and efficiency of modern economies but also create space for economic inclusivity and transformation efforts. The universal basic income emerges as a progressive line of thought in economic discourse, designed to address issues of wage stagnation and job displacement due to automation and globalization. UBI could redistribute the benefits gained technologically, making societal structures more resilient and equitable.

With this groundwork laid, the next section will explore universal basic income more deeply. We'll examine its promise as a tool not just for financial relief, but also as a potential catalyst for societal change. By fostering an environment where citizens are cushioned against economic turbulence, UBI might not just supplement incomes but also stimulate overall economic activity and innovation. This discussion will continue by assessing the values and economic theories supporting UBI, offering a clearer picture of how this initiative could redefine economic and social landscapes in concert with the evolving paradigm brought forth by CBDCs.

Exploring the Potential for Universal Basic Income

As we shift from previous discussions on the significant role of Central Bank Digital Currencies (CBDCs) in future monetary systems, the conversation naturally leads us to consider universal basic income (UBI) as a complementary innovation. CBDCs aim to enhance transaction transparency and tackle some of the cybersecurity risks that come with digital transactions. These developments lay a potent groundwork for economic reforms like UBI, aimed at revolutionizing how we handle economic equity.

UBI introduces the concept of distributing a regular, unconditional amount of money to all citizens. Advocates argue that this could transform societal structures by ensuring that everyone has a baseline of economic security. Imagine a world where everyone receives a stable income, regardless of employment status. This floor of financial security could unlock innovation, creativity, and entrepreneurship by reducing the stress associated with meeting basic needs. The potential impact is vast, influencing everything from individual well-being to national economic health.

Concrete examples of UBI in practice provide insight into its transformative power. Finland's two-year experiment, though limited in scope, gives a glimpse of its potential. Between 2017 and 2018, the Finnish government provided a randomized group of unemployed citizens with a monthly income with no strings attached. Participants reported improved well-being and less stress, though critics pointed out employment effects were less clear-cut. Still, it demonstrated how UBI can alleviate financial anxiety, offering greater freedom to pursue meaningful work.

Another promising example comes from Stockton, California, where a smaller-scale program provided selected residents $500 per month. Early results echoed those from Finland, with participants experiencing reduced income volatility, better health, and

increased ability to secure full-time work. When people are not constantly worried about their next meal or rent, they tend to contribute more positively to society.
Countries like Kenya are exploring even more ambitious UBI pilots. In Kenya, a long-term pilot managed by the organization GiveDirectly is set in motion with plans to span over a decade. The aim is to study impacts over a longer horizon, assessing how a reliable income affects various aspects of life, from children's education to adults' health and productivity.

While these examples highlight UBI's promising facets, the concept also presents challenges. Funding is a significant hurdle, requiring governments to reconsider taxation systems and redistribute resources on a potentially massive scale. UBI forces a re-evaluation of existing welfare systems. It may streamline bureaucracy by eliminating means-testing and numerous conditional programs, which could lead to cost savings. However, policymakers must carefully design these transitions to ensure that vulnerable populations do not fall through the cracks during reform.
Labor market impacts are another area of concern. Critics argue UBI might disincentivize work, but evidence from pilots suggests people often continue working, albeit in roles better aligned with their skills and interests. By removing the pressure of low-paid, unstable jobs, UBI may encourage retraining and education, ultimately leading to a more skilled workforce. It promotes better matching between jobs and workers, potentially boosting productivity and job satisfaction.

In examining UBI's effects on societal well-being, we can anticipate benefits that ripple through communities. With financial security, individuals can afford healthy food and healthcare, reducing long-term public health costs. Education might see a boost as families can invest more in their children's futures, a shift that could pay dividends in higher skilled future generations. Community engagement might flourish as people have more time and means to participate in civic life.
To remain inclusive, UBI needs robust policy design to cater to diverse populations. Variations in living costs mean one size will not fit all. Urban centers might require higher payments than rural areas due to cost discrepancies. Policymakers need to address these nuances to ensure equitable distribution across different regions and communities.
Lessons from current welfare models might inform UBI design, hinting at possible synergies. Current schemes target specific needs, often inefficiently. In contrast, UBI promises simplicity and inclusivity, addressing poverty by delivering funds to everyone. However, reassessing welfare systems requires political will and public buy-in. Equitable resource distribution hinges on public acceptance of shared prosperity principles.

As we contemplate a seamless transition to future topics, it's clear that technological advancements like CBDCs and socio-economic tools like UBI lay fertile ground for innovative economic models. These models could drive more equitable resource allocation, providing societies with the resilience needed to face an uncertain future. By investing in systems that promote financial inclusion, we might craft an economy that values well-being over wealth concentration, uniting technology and policy in common cause for a better tomorrow.

Discussion of New Economic Models
Coming off our talk about Universal Basic Income (UBI), we see its potential to offer

financial stability. This aligns well with the emerging Central Bank Digital Currencies (CBDCs). At first glance, you might wonder how these two concepts connect, but look closer. Both aim to reshape how we think about economic equality and stability.
UBI offers a consistent financial cushion that can help level the playing field, breaking the traditional chains that bind us to unequal systems of wealth distribution. Introducing digital currencies could serve as an efficient and transparent underpinning for this. CBDCs streamline the transaction process, making it more cost-effective and accessible to everyone, not just to those fortunate enough to navigate or manipulate the current financial labyrinth.
Think about traditional banking. It is often laden with fees, time delays, and geographical constraints. People in rural areas or developing countries might find it especially hard to access banking services. The economic playing field is thus inherently slanted. CBDCs hold the promise of universal access. You could imagine a vendor in a remote village conducting transactions with the same efficiency and security as someone in a major city. Devices like smartphones can act as gateways to these advanced economic models.

The privacy concerns that accompany digital activities are real, but they do not outweigh the benefits in this case. Blockchain technologies and cryptographic protocols can ensure that digital currencies do not jeopardize privacy or security. Countries like China have already launched pilot programs for digital currencies, suggesting that other nations will soon follow suit. Picture a world where money flows as easily and freely as text messages. This might sound utopian, but it is not far-fetched.
When these digital wallets become a norm, even small transactions gain unprecedented transparency, more than we ever expected from traditional currencies. This could work wonders for reducing corruption. Imagine governments allocating budgets or distributing aid through CBDCs—every single transaction is traceable, making it much harder for funds to disappear into bureaucratic black holes.
A more balanced and inclusive economic landscape isn't just about equitable distribution. It's also about sustainable economic practices that include everyone. CBDCs offer speed and flexibility in financial operations. Government-issued digital money could simplify tax collection, dramatically reducing bureaucratic costs and delays. This, in turn, could enable governments to reallocate funds to strategic areas like education or healthcare, sectors that touch our daily lives.

So, how do these technologies reimagine resource allocation? Think of them as enforcers of economic integrity. Even well-meaning policies can falter under the weight of inefficient deployment. Governments can ensure targeted financial assistance without it being siphoned off by intermediaries. Direct transfers enabled by digital currencies could also optimize resource allocation, addressing some of our more glaring economic challenges. For those in precarious living conditions, immediate access to funds means immediate alleviation of hardship, even if just a bit. This direct aid can help stabilize families, communities, and by extension, entire economies.
Next, let us examine how CBDCs might redefine economic interactions. Today's financial systems resemble a crowded highway, clogged and slow. Transactions need verification and validation from multiple parties. Cryptographic checks built into CBDCs would remove much of this friction. Money could flow more freely between individuals, businesses, and governments, igniting economic interactions that fuel growth. Imagine

the gig economy, bustling but disorganized at times, receiving a jolt of structure and efficiency thanks to CBDCs. Freelancers can conduct transactions with clients globally in real-time, with minimal fees.

Another possibility is the rise of smart contracts, agreements embedded within digital currencies themselves. These can automatically validate terms once conditions are met, making transactions more efficient and less dependent on human oversight. Picture booking services or renting properties without the need for a middleman. These innovations bring unprecedented efficiency to sectors ranging from real estate to everyday consumer transactions.

CBDCs also stand to revolutionize cross-border transactions. Current systems involve currency conversion fees and processing delays that often discourage international efforts. Central Bank Digital Currencies can facilitate seamless exchanges, potentially boosting international trade and partnerships.

As you can see, CBDCs contribute to an inclusive economic landscape, addressing societal inequalities. They provide means to disrupt entrenched structures that hold people back. With access to digital currencies, financial literacy will also need to improve. Governments and institutions must aim for awareness programs to help citizens understand these new systems. If people learn how to use this technology effectively, the gap between technological savviness and economic participation narrows.

Long-term societal transformation might sound grand, but that is the crux of what these innovations represent. They bear the promise of altering entrenched habits, rising above outdated models limiting our potential. It is essential that, along with these advancements, our policies resonate with the challenges of contemporary digital economies. The way people engage with these emerging systems will help define the political and social narrative of the future.

Investing in the infrastructure to support CBDCs might seem like a hefty investment. Yet, structured correctly, it could replace aged, inefficient systems costing more in long-term mismanagement. Expense notwithstanding, this promises returns, not just financially but socially as well. We are not going to find a cure-all in these technologies. However, they offer a pathway that, when taken responsibly, allows societies to break away from structural inequalities.

To see these changes as mere financial tweaks does them a disservice. They represent technological shifts supporting a fairer, more inclusive economic landscape. If implemented thoughtfully, the synergy between UBI and CBDCs can lead the way to societies fostering equality, innovation, and sustainability—goals that seem distant now but need not remain so.

Without doubt, the merging of Universal Basic Income with Central Bank Digital Currencies offers a compelling vision of future economic models. As we stand on the brink of digital currency becoming mainstream, we need to remain both optimistic and vigilant. Could this be the dawn of a new economic era? The answer lies not just in technological possibilities but in how society chooses to engage with them.

Final Insights

As we explore the transformative potential of Central Bank Digital Currencies (CBDCs) and universal basic income (UBI), it's clear these innovations can reshape economic landscapes by promoting greater inclusivity and efficiency. CBDCs simplify and secure transactions, potentially making financial access easy for everyone, while UBI ensures a stable income for all citizens, fostering economic security and creativity. Together, they challenge traditional banking models and offer a roadmap toward a more equitable financial future. With CBDCs' real-time transparency and UBI's promise of unconditional support, we stand on the brink of new economic systems that prioritize well-being over wealth disparity. This journey involves careful design and public engagement to harness these technologies responsibly and equitably. Now that we understand their capabilities, we can anticipate exciting opportunities to redefine how money works globally, impacting everything from individual livelihoods to international trade dynamics. As societies transition into this digital era, keeping an eye on technological progress while addressing privacy and cybersecurity concerns will be crucial in shaping a fairer, sustainable, and resilient economy for everyone.

Chapter 13: *How to Get Started with Crypto*

Have you ever felt completely overwhelmed by new technology, unsure of where to even begin? You're not alone. Many people feel this way when they first hear about cryptocurrency. The concept of digital coins and blockchain can seem like a daunting puzzle. Some might wonder if they have to be tech wizards just to understand how it all works. There's also the fear of security risks and scams that comes with entering unfamiliar territory. These feelings of uncertainty can make stepping into the crypto world seem intimidating.

But what if diving in wasn't as complex as it seems? This chapter is designed to address those very questions, offering clear and practical guidance on safely starting your journey with cryptocurrency. By demystifying the essentials, we aim to empower you with the knowledge needed to navigate this exciting digital landscape confidently.

Introduction to Crypto for Beginners

Cryptocurrency represents a revolutionary leap in how we perceive and use money. At its core, cryptocurrency is a digital or virtual form of currency that employs cryptography to secure transactions, control new units creation, and verify asset transfers. This foundation rests within a decentralized digital ledger known as blockchain. The concept of decentralization plays a pivotal role here. Traditionally, currencies depend on centralized institutions like banks to regulate and facilitate transactions. Cryptocurrency, however, disrupts this paradigm by allowing transactions to occur directly between individuals without intermediaries, ting back to the backbone technology: blockchain. Blockchain serves as a distributed database composed of blocks that are cryptographically secured against tampering. Picture it this way: every transaction is a new entry in a massive digital ledger. This virtual ledger isn't stored in one location. Everyone connected to the network holds a copy, making it virtually impossible to alter any information without everyone noticing. This transparency builds trust among users because they can verify every transaction's history, and immutability ensures that once data enters the blockchain, it's there for good.

A key aspect of engaging with cryptocurrencies is understanding differing currencies. Bitcoin, often dubbed the first cryptocurrency, laid the foundation for blockchain technology as we know it. It's renowned for being limited in supply, akin to precious commodities like gold. This gives it value potential beyond mere transaction facilitation. Altcoins, or alternative cryptocurrencies, vary in their applications and structures. Ethereum, for example, introduced the concept of smart contracts—self-executing contracts with terms written into code. This innovation allows for decentralized applications, or DApps, essentially programs running on the blockchain without interference or downtime.

Stablecoins represent another category, presenting an anchor of stability in the volatile crypto seas. They're pegged to traditional assets like the US dollar or gold, making them a viable choice for regular transactions. For instance, if someone wants to transact in cryptocurrency without worrying about market fluctuations, using a stablecoin provides the benefits of crypto with reduced risk. These distinctions between Bitcoin, altcoins like Ethereum, and stablecoins form a crucial backbone to understanding the broader crypto

landscape.
Cryptocurrencies present real-world applications that resonate universally. Imagine a family member is working abroad. Traditional bank transfers take several days and incur high fees. Sending Bitcoin can significantly reduce time and cost constraints in such remittances. Another scenario features Ethereum, where through smart contracts, businesses automate complex processes like supply chain management, reducing delays and errors. These examples underscore cryptocurrencies' potential to reshape existing frameworks across industries.

Misconceptions often cloud understanding cryptocurrencies. Many people equate Bitcoin with all cryptocurrencies, a generalization that hinders recognizing the full potential of other coins with distinct advantages. Regulators worry about the anonymous nature of transactions leading to illicit activities. While it's vital to consider these concerns, it's equally crucial to acknowledge advancements like know-your-customer (KYC) and anti-money laundering (AML) protocols, increasing legitimacy within the crypto space. Educating oneself helps navigate these nuances and apprehend credible information amidst widespread myths.
Navigating the expansive world of cryptocurrencies requires diligence and a proactive approach. Blockchain brings profound security advantages but isn't infallible against user negligence. Users need to exercise caution in interactions, safeguarding themselves against common digital threats. With great potential comes the responsibility of informed usage.

The conversation around cryptocurrency naturally extends to acquisition—how does one actually obtain it, and where does one start? This entails selecting platforms, known as exchanges, where one can trade traditional money for cryptocurrency. Exchanges vary widely, with some offering a broad range of currency options, others specializing in specific coins. Establishing an account with proof of identity forms the next step, followed by purchasing coins. Securing these digital assets is imperative, typically achieved by transferring them to a wallet.
Wallets range from hardware devices resembling USB sticks to digital applications, both designed to safely store cryptocurrency keys. Consider them your personal vault for digital assets. This ensures that even if an exchange is compromised, your funds remain secured outside its environment. Readers must ensure familiarity with these critical steps to prevent potential security breaches.
In transitioning focus to acquiring cryptocurrency, understanding the intertwined nature of its facets sets the stage efficiently. The next section will delve into practicalities, from choosing exchanges and creating accounts to purchasing coins and securely storing them in wallets. The goal is to empower readers with actionable steps toward participating in the crypto world.

Recognizing the curiosity, excitement, and trepidation accompanying cryptocurrency exploration confirms the need for accessible knowledge. Equipping yourself with clarity on foundational aspects not only informs decisions but encourages meaningful engagement devoid of unwarranted fears. The digital currency realm isn't just a niche market for tech enthusiasts; its implications span global economics, influencing how money is perceived culturally and practically. Keeping an open mind to its extensive effects, while staying informed on continual advancements, ultimately enhances your journey into digital currencies.

Every point serves toward strengthening the knowledge foundation for prospective endeavors. By connecting these details comprehensively, you unravel a complex topic into digestible insights applicable in everyday scenarios. Delving into acquiring crypto fosters engagement, drawing readers deeper into the crypto sphere, where each successive layer reveals innovative possibilities shaped by you and enabled through blockchain.

Understanding How to Buy and Store Cryptocurrency

To explore the world of cryptocurrencies, you need to be equipped with fundamental knowledge about what these digital assets are and how they work. Cryptocurrencies are digital or virtual currencies that use cryptography for security, and they operate on decentralized networks based on blockchain technology. Different types exist, from the well-known Bitcoin to alternatives like Ethereum, Ripple, and Litecoin, each with unique functionalities. This foundation is critical for navigating the practical steps of acquiring cryptocurrency.

First, selecting a cryptocurrency exchange is your gateway to buying cryptocurrencies. Consider factors like user-friendliness, transaction fees, and security features. Popular exchanges include Coinbase, Binance, and Kraken, but your choice should depend on personal priorities and regional availability. An exchange with an easy-to-navigate platform and competitive fees can simplify your crypto journey. Equally important is security. Look for exchanges that enforce strong regulatory measures and security protocols, such as two-factor authentication and cold storage for user funds.

Once you've picked an exchange, creating an account is your next step. This involves filling out basic information and verifying your identity, which might include submitting government-issued identification and proof of address. This process, known as Know Your Customer (KYC), is essential for complying with regulations and safeguarding your account. Pay careful attention to provide correct details to avoid verification delays, which could lead to frustrating transaction hold-ups.

With your account verified, you're ready to make your first cryptocurrency purchase. Start by deciding which coins to buy. Bitcoin could be a solid initial choice due to its stability, but exploring coins like Ethereum, known for smart contracts, could be beneficial too. Determine the amount you want to purchase based on your investment goal and risk tolerance. Understand transaction types like 'market order,' which executes the transaction at the current market rate, or 'limit order,' which allows you to set a specific price. This knowledge empowers you to make informed purchase decisions.

To carry out a transaction securely, ensure that the internet connection you're using is secure, preferably from a private network. Once you've acquired the cryptocurrencies, consider the best storage practice. A common misconception is that they're stored on exchanges indefinitely; in reality, this comes with risks. Solutions like software wallets, hardware wallets, and paper wallets offer safer alternatives, each with pros and cons. Software wallets provide convenient access but require strong passwords and encrypted backups. Hardware wallets, like Ledger and Trezor, offer enhanced security by keeping your private keys offline. Despite being a physical device, they must be safeguarded against loss. Paper wallets, which involve printing your keys, eliminate digital threats but need protection from physical harm.

Setting up your chosen wallet type demands careful attention to securing private keys and backup phrases, crucial to recovering your assets if access is lost. This step cannot be overstated; mismanagement here can lead to irrecoverable loss. Use secure methods to store digital copies and keep physical copies in safe locations, such as a safe or bank deposit box, to shield them from unforeseen events.

As the landscape of cryptocurrencies evolves, so does the complexity of ensuring secure transactions and storage. Investing time in understanding safe storage practices serves as an investment in the security of your digital assets. This topic transitions seamlessly to the importance of security in cryptocurrency dealings. Incorporating simple yet effective safety measures like enabling two-factor authentication fortifies your account against unauthorized access. Recognizing phishing attempts helps protect your assets from cyber threats.

These security protocols safeguard your investments and maintain the integrity of your cryptocurrency journey. They set the stage for the subsequent discussion, focusing on specific strategies to enhance security. Activating two-factor authentication, being vigilant against phishing, and understanding the vital role of protecting private keys are necessary defenses against digital threats. Cryptocurrency ownership comes with the constant responsibility of being a steward of your security.

In summary, entering the world of cryptocurrencies doesn't have to be a daunting endeavor. By following these outlined steps—choosing a reputable exchange, setting up your account, purchasing wisely, and securing your assets with appropriate storage solutions—you can embark on your crypto adventures with confidence and caution. The landscape is rich with opportunities, but it demands respect for the practices and protocols that ensure safety and sustainability. As you delve deeper into cryptocurrency management, the forthcoming section will delve into advanced security measures, equipping you with the knowledge to navigate potential risks with heightened awareness and preparedness.

Explanation of Safety Measures for New Users

In this digital age, as you start your cryptocurrency journey, you've already taken the initial steps to acquire some coins. Now, it’s time to shift focus towards securing those investments. Think of it like locking the door of your house before leaving. It's vital in ensuring that your digital assets remain yours and yours alone.

A critical first step to securing your cryptocurrency is enabling two-factor authentication (2FA). Imagine 2FA as adding an extra lock to your digital vault. It's more than just a password. It's a second layer of security that could stop unauthorized access. One common 2FA method is using an authenticator app like Google Authenticator. When you log in, it requires a code generated by the app, something only you can access from your phone. There's also the option of SMS-based 2FA, where you'll receive a text message with a code. However, this method can be less secure due to SIM card swapping attacks. By enabling 2FA, you effectively add a formidable barrier to your crypto accounts.

Yet, while you fortify your defenses, you must also be aware of phishing attempts—deceptive tactics used by cyber criminals to trick you into revealing sensitive information. Picture receiving an email that looks identical to one from your exchange, urgently asking you to click a link and verify your account. However convincing it seems, this is likely a phishing attempt. Always scrutinize such emails for signs of deception, like unusual sender addresses or poor grammar. Never click on unknown links or share your private information. By staying vigilant, you mitigate the risk of unauthorized access to your accounts.

Besides external threats, you must also focus on safeguarding your private keys. These keys are crucial as they give access to your cryptocurrency. Think of them as the master keys to your digital safe. If lost or stolen, regaining access is nearly impossible. For instance, storing your private keys offline on a hardware wallet shields them from online threats. If you opt to write them down, keep them in a secure place, like a safe or deposit box. This way, you ensure that your digital assets are protected and accessible only to you. Losing a private key often means losing the assets tied to it, which could be a costly mistake.

To further bolster your digital assets' security, explore different types of digital wallets available. Hot wallets, which are connected to the internet, can be useful for day-to-day transactions but are more vulnerable to attacks. Conversely, cold wallets, which remain offline, offer enhanced security at the expense of convenience. For long-term storage, cold wallets are often recommended. Opting for reputable wallet providers ensures an additional layer of trustworthiness and reduces the risk of vulnerabilities.

Apart from choosing the right wallet, ensure you have reliable backup options. Consider applications that permit backup and recovery of your wallet in the event of a hardware failure or loss. You wouldn't want to find yourself in a position where technical issues lead to loss of access. By regularly updating backups, you prepare yourself for unforeseen circumstances while keeping your investments intact.

As you weave these security measures into your routine, you're laying a foundation of trust and security. Why are these actions essential? With cryptocurrencies, while promising, come risks that act as deterrents to newcomers. Your path into this world grows more arduous without such safeguards. Implementing these strategies demonstrates diligence and responsibility, qualities necessary for success in the rapidly evolving digital currency landscape.

Keeping these security measures in mind also prepares you for the next chapter of your crypto journey, where we'll explore long-term investment strategies. Balancing security with insight and foresight becomes crucial as we delve into understanding market volatility, setting realistic goals, and diversifying your crypto portfolio. These strategies ensure you're not only protecting your assets but also enhancing them.

By concentrating on maintaining a secure environment for your digital assets, you pave the way for exploring and optimizing investments. Such practices cultivate a space where security and profitability can thrive together. As you master these concepts, your confidence in handling cryptocurrencies will grow, dispelling initial uncertainties and empowering you to make informed decisions that benefit your digital future.

Moving forward, let's shift gears and consider how understanding market trends, setting personal financial goals, and diversifying your investment can help manage risks and maximize opportunities. These components are vital as you gain a deeper grasp of the crypto realm. Together, we'll navigate the complexities and rewards it offers, ensuring you're well-equipped to harness its potential safely and effectively.

Developing a Sustainable Investment Strategy in Crypto

Safety is the bedrock of any cryptocurrency endeavor. As users secure their assets through measures like two-factor authentication and vigilant monitoring against phishing, the preparation for future growth begins. Building on this foundation is crucial, because after securing what one has, the natural progression is to plan for what one wants to achieve. This chapter guides us into the next phase—establishing a long-term investment plan.

Setting realistic goals ranks high in importance. Goals grounded in reality provide clarity and direction. The crypto market, unlike traditional investments, is known for its thrills and spills, so understanding one's financial capacity and desired outcomes is essential from the get-go. For example, a beginner entering this realm might aim to grow their initial investment by a modest percentage over a year. This is more practical and attainable than hoping for a fortune overnight.

Market volatility is as much a part of crypto as are blockchain and ledgers. It can seem daunting at first, but with the right approach, one can navigate these choppy waters. Drawing parallels with weather forecasting can help. Meteorologists can't always pinpoint exact weather conditions for a future date, but they can prepare us with probabilities and trends. Similarly, crypto investors can't predict exact market moves, but they can use historical data, news events, and market trends to make educated guesses. This understanding allows them to make timely decisions in line with their investment strategy.

Diversifying a crypto portfolio is as critical as understanding the assets themselves. It's like not putting all eggs in one basket. Diversification is about managing risk, balancing potential losses with potential gains. An investor might choose to hold a mix of established cryptocurrencies like Bitcoin and Ethereum alongside promising altcoins. Bitcoin, often dubbed 'digital gold', provides a relatively stable base, while Ethereum, with its smart contract functionality, adds a different layer of growth potential. Meanwhile, altcoins offer possibilities for high returns, albeit with higher risks. By spreading investments across these categories, the impact of any one asset's poor performance is reduced.

For example, consider the story of Jane, a new investor who wisely divides her portfolio across various types of cryptocurrencies. She allocates 50% to Bitcoin, 30% to Ethereum, and 20% to a mix of altcoins like Cardano and Solana. When an unexpected market dip affects her altcoins, the stability provided by Bitcoin and the strong network being built for Ethereum help cushion the blow. The diversity in her investment strategy helps her maintain relative stability, allowing her to stay the course when the unexpected happens.

This approach stands in stark contrast to a single-asset holding, which could dramatically decrease an investor's portfolio during downturns. Diversification mitigates such risks and promotes a more balanced investment journey.

As you journey into the crypto world armed with these strategies, remember the power of continuous education. Markets evolve, technologies advance, and with them, opportunities change. Keeping abreast of these shifts ensures that one's investment plan doesn't stagnate. Recently emerged platforms or new partnerships within the blockchain universe might present new investment opportunities. Staying informed allows you to adjust your strategy in response to these changes.

Engaging with the broader community—online forums, social media groups, and webinars—can also provide valuable insights. Community insights, when scrutinized critically, might offer unconventional perspectives or early signals about shifts in market sentiment. Following credible voices and experts who analyze trends can supplement

one's understanding and preparedness.
While a solid investment foundation is necessary, we'll delve into maintaining these investments next. It's not only about making informed choices initially; it's about actively managing one's portfolio over time. This includes tracking portfolio performance, rebalancing assets depending on the shifting market landscape, and understanding the timing for buying or selling holdings. These ongoing actions are crucial for sustaining growth and minimizing losses.

Implementing a long-term strategy requires the discipline to adhere to one's plan amidst the noise of daily price swings and the temptation to chase short-lived trends. Discipline aids in tuning out distractions and focusing on the end goals—a crucial quality that distinguishes successful investors from the rest.
In this ever-evolving space, adaptability remains a key trait. A strategy that works today might need tweaking tomorrow. Your future might include exploring other financial instruments like NFTs or staking for passive income. Remember, flexibility to incorporate new strategies aligns with the dynamism of the crypto market.
Before wrapping up this discussion, let's not forget to celebrate small victories. Achieving a milestone, no matter how minor, contributes to the investor's journey. Whether it's reaching a savings goal or successfully navigating market fluctuations without panic-selling, acknowledge these accomplishments as they reinforce the benefits of planning and perseverance.
Our upcoming section will explore strategies for effectively tracking portfolio performance. Understanding your returns, reassessing goals, and making timely adjustments keep your investment plan viable. Engaging tools and software are available that simplify these tasks, offering real-time insights and suggesting when it might be time to rebalance portfolios or cash out. With the knowledge acquired today, you'll be better equipped to adapt to and thrive in the dynamic world of cryptocurrency.

Lifecycle Management of a Crypto Portfolio

In the dynamic world of cryptocurrency, simply setting up a portfolio isn't the end of the journey—it's the beginning. Previously, we discussed long-term strategies such as setting realistic goals and managing risk through diversification. The question now is: How do you maintain and adjust your crypto investments as conditions change? This question narrows our focus to understanding the significance of active portfolio management. Let's explore what this means for sustaining a successful crypto journey.
Imagine your investment being like a garden. You don't just plant seeds and walk away. You water them, make sure they get sunlight, and pull out any weeds that pop up. Your crypto investments need similar care. One of the essential tools for this is portfolio tracking. Consider apps like Blockfolio or Delta. These apps help you keep a pulse on your investments, showing you real-time stats. Imagine being able to check how each asset in your portfolio is performing at any moment. This kind of insight empowers you to make informed decisions.
Now, let's talk about rebalancing. This concept is about bringing your portfolio back to its intended state. Say you've decided you want 60% of your investments in Bitcoin, 30% in Ethereum, and 10% in smaller altcoins. Over time, the value of these assets will fluctuate. Suddenly, Bitcoin might outperform, or Ethereum might dip. Your portfolio could end up looking more like 70% Bitcoin, 20% Ethereum, and 10% altcoins. This is when rebalancing comes into play. By selling some Bitcoin and buying Ethereum, you

bring your investments back to your original plan.

This approach not only helps stabilize your investment according to your risk tolerance but also encourages the habit of "buying low and selling high" without second-guessing or market timing. Maintaining the plan helps you stay grounded in a market known for its volatility. Real-life examples underscore this—a study cited by financial experts often shows portfolios that are regularly rebalanced tend to have better risk-adjusted returns over time.

Every crypto user sooner or later learns the market's unpredictable nature. Keeping an eye on trends is crucial, and not just in the major currencies. One aspect of adapting to market changes is recognizing when to diversify into new or emerging assets. The tech world is brimming with innovation, and the crypto sphere is no different. New tokens, forks of existing coins, or entirely new blockchain technologies regularly emerge. While it's tempting to chase every trend, grounding yourself in research remains essential. Platforms like CoinMarketCap and communities on Reddit can provide valuable insights into potential tech advances or market shifts.

But how do you know when to adapt? A practical approach is setting alerts or thresholds. For instance, if a particular coin's value changes by more than a certain percentage within a set time, that's your cue to investigate and decide if action is needed. Modern apps and platforms often feature such alert systems, and they can act as your early warning radar, ensuring you're always a step ahead.

Education is another vital piece to this puzzle. The more you understand the underlying technology of cryptocurrency, the more equipped you are to spot trends and adapt solutions. For instance, knowing the impact of a blockchain fork can help you predict how a coin's value might change. Engaging with crypto communities or enrolling in online courses can enhance your understanding. Popular platforms like Coursera or educational channels on YouTube can break down complex ideas into simpler concepts. They offer a pathway to better understand blockchain technology, tokenomics, and more.

Creating a sustainable strategy involves not just focusing on the present but preparing for the future. Consider how regulatory changes can influence your investments. Countries around the world are still figuring out how to regulate cryptocurrency, with rules varying greatly from one jurisdiction to another. Staying informed on these trends can save you from potential pitfalls. Following discussions in online forums or subscribing to news outlets can help you keep your ear to the ground. Many crypto enthusiasts recommend resources like CoinDesk for keeping up to date with major regulatory shifts.

Think also about security, a perennial topic in the crypto world. As you adjust your portfolio, never lose sight of protecting your digital assets. Making use of cold wallets, two-factor authentication, and regular password updates are non-negotiable best practices. Picture your portfolio like a treasure chest; even the most valuable gems can vanish without adequate protection. Even if you have the best strategy in place, poor security can undermine everything.

Let's get a bit personal here. Psychological resilience matters too. Crypto investing isn't just numbers and catchy headlines—it's an emotional rollercoaster. Emotional ups and downs can cloud judgment, nudging one to make impulsive moves. Practicing discipline and patience are your best companions. Think back on the foundation we spoke about, setting goals that aren't just about making profits but also about maintaining peace of mind. This is where communities can be quite supportive. Engaging with other investors on platforms like Twitter or Discord can offer camaraderie and different perspectives, helping manage the stress and excitement that comes with crypto investing.

Every step you take, from tracking your portfolio to studying the markets and protecting your assets with security measures, forms a part of your journey towards mastering crypto investing. It's not just about riding the waves but learning to navigate through them with informed decisions. By staying vigilant, educated, and connected, you'll be better equipped to cultivate and nurture a crypto portfolio that thrives in an ever-changing landscape.

Concluding Thoughts

By embarking on this crypto journey with a solid understanding of safety and practicality, you're not only safeguarding your assets but also setting the stage for sustainable growth and exploration. The comprehensive knowledge gained from choosing exchanges, making informed purchases, and securing your digital assets equips you to confidently engage with the evolving landscape of cryptocurrency. As you continue forward, let curiosity guide you through deeper explorations of investment strategies and emerging technologies. Embrace this dynamic world with vigilance and adaptability, as the opportunities within digital finance are vast and ever-changing. Your responsible approach today paves the way for successful integration into a future where cryptocurrency plays an integral role in personal and economic development.

A NEW ERA
OF EMPOWERMENT
FINANCIAL
INCLUSION
Cryptocurrency provides financial access to unberserved communities
ECONOMIC
OPPORTUNITY
It enables people to participate in the global economy and generate income
INNOVATIVE
SOLUTIONS
Advancements in finance and technology are driving social change

Conclusion:

As we stand at the edge of a financial revolution, it's clear that cryptocurrency is more than just a technological innovation — it's a movement. A movement that empowers individuals, decentralizes control, and opens access to opportunities once reserved for a privileged few.

Crypto is about inclusion. It's about giving the unbanked a voice, creating wealth pathways outside traditional systems, and sparking innovation in places where hope once seemed scarce.

For me, this book isn't just a guide. It's a **mission** — to demystify the world of digital currency, to break down barriers of entry, and to light a path for anyone willing to take the first step toward financial literacy and independence.

A Call to Action: Embrace, Educate, and Empower

Embrace the technology. Learn how it works. Understand the principles.

Educate yourself and others. Share your knowledge. Uplift your community.

Empower the future. Use this tool to create change — personal, professional, and societal.

This is more than an investment trend — it's a shift in power, mindset, and potential.

Your journey starts now.

With clarity, courage, and commitment,
— ***Derrick Sekiziyivu***
Certified Digital Finance Practitioner
Founder, Tazzuba.com

Glossary of crypto terms

A–C

Address: A string of letters and numbers used to send and receive cryptocurrency (like a digital bank account number).

Altcoin: Any cryptocurrency other than Bitcoin (e.g., Ethereum, Litecoin).

AML (Anti-Money Laundering): Laws and regulations aimed at preventing illegal use of cryptocurrencies.

Blockchain: A decentralized digital ledger that records transactions across a network of computers.

CBDC (Central Bank Digital Currency): Digital currency issued by a government's central bank.

Cold Wallet: A crypto wallet that is offline, offering greater security from hacks.

D–F

Decentralization: Distribution of authority away from a central figure or institution.

DeFi (Decentralized Finance): Financial services built on blockchain that operate without banks or brokers.

Digital Gold: A term used to describe Bitcoin's role as a store of value, like gold.

DApp (Decentralized Application): Apps that run on a blockchain rather than a centralized server.

Fork: A split in a blockchain that creates a new version of the chain (can be soft or hard).

Fiat Currency: Government-issued currency not backed by a physical commodity (e.g., USD, EUR).

G–L

Gas Fees: Small payments users make to perform transactions on blockchain platforms like Ethereum.

HODL: A slang term for "hold," referring to keeping crypto rather than selling.

Hot Wallet: A wallet connected to the internet, convenient but more vulnerable to hacking.

Hash: A unique string of numbers and letters generated by a hash function — essential for blockchain security.

KYC (Know Your Customer): Identity verification process used by exchanges to prevent fraud.

M–P

Mining: The process of validating blockchain transactions and earning rewards in the form of new coins.

NFT (Non-Fungible Token): Unique digital assets that represent ownership of specific items, such as art or music.

Node: A computer that participates in a blockchain network by maintaining a copy of the ledger.

Private Key: A secure code that grants access to your cryptocurrency — never share this.

Public Key: A code that others use to send you cryptocurrency.

R–T

Smart Contract: Self-executing code on the blockchain that performs actions when conditions are met.

Stablecoin: A type of cryptocurrency pegged to a stable asset like USD, reducing price volatility.

Satoshi: The smallest unit of Bitcoin (0.00000001 BTC), named after Bitcoin's creator.

Token: A digital asset built on top of a blockchain (e.g., ERC-20 tokens on Ethereum).

Transaction Fee: A small amount paid to miners or validators to process a transaction.

U–Z

Utility Token: A token that provides access to a product or service on a blockchain platform.

Volatility: The rate at which the price of a cryptocurrency changes — often high in crypto markets.

Wallet: A digital tool for storing, sending, and receiving cryptocurrency.

Whale: An individual or entity that holds a large amount of cryptocurrency.

White Paper: A document that outlines the purpose, technology, and roadmap of a crypto project.

Resources for further learning

Websites & Platforms

CoinDesk
Leading news site for blockchain and crypto updates, analysis, and data.

CoinMarketCap
Real-time prices, market capitalization, and info on thousands of cryptocurrencies.

CryptoCompare
Tools for tracking portfolio, coins, and exchange reviews.

Blockchain.com Explorer
Track real-time Bitcoin transactions and wallet balances.

Ethereum.org
Official website for Ethereum — offers developer guides, wallet advice, and beginner material.

Books

The Bitcoin Standard by **Saifedean Ammous**
A deep dive into Bitcoin's economic implications and monetary theory.

Digital Gold by **Nathaniel Popper**
Chronicles the early history of Bitcoin and its pioneers.

Mastering Bitcoin by **Andreas M. Antonopoulos**
A must-read for those wanting a technical understanding of Bitcoin and blockchain.

Cryptoassets by **Chris Burniske & Jack Tatar**
A guide to evaluating and investing in digital assets.

Courses & Learning Platforms

Coursera: Bitcoin and Cryptocurrency Technologies (Princeton)
Free course explaining the technical side of crypto.

Udemy: Cryptocurrency Investment Course 2024: Fund Your Retirement!
An investment-focused course ideal for beginners.

Khan Academy – Bitcoin Series
Animated and easy-to-understand videos on how Bitcoin works.

Communities & Forums
Reddit: r/CryptoCurrency
Massive community for discussion, news, and advice.

BitcoinTalk.org
The oldest crypto forum, founded by Satoshi Nakamoto.

[Twitter (X)]

Follow crypto thought leaders like:
@APompliano (Anthony Pompliano)
@balajis (Balaji Srinivasan)
@saylor (Michael Saylor)
@aantonop (Andreas Antonopoulos)

Crypto Tools & Trackers
MetaMask – Browser wallet for Ethereum and tokens.

Ledger – Hardware wallet for cold storage.

Glassnode – On-chain analytics platform.

CoinGecko – Alternative to CoinMarketCap with extensive data.

Inspiring crypto success stories

From Homeless to Bitcoin Millionaire – Erik Finman

At just 12 years old, Erik Finman invested $1,000 (gifted by his grandmother) in Bitcoin when it was priced at around $12. By age 18, his holdings had grown to over $4 million. Once labeled a struggling student, Erik leveraged crypto's rise to become a teenage millionaire, later launching education-focused ventures and advocating for financial literacy through crypto.

Crypto Saving Lives in Venezuela

In hyperinflation-struck Venezuela, cryptocurrency became a *lifeline*. Citizens began turning to Bitcoin and stablecoins to preserve value and access global markets, bypassing government currency controls. Many used crypto to receive remittances, buy groceries, and even pay for medical care. Platforms like **Binance** and **LocalBitcoins** became vital for survival.

Paxful's Peer-to-Peer Impact in Africa

Paxful, a peer-to-peer Bitcoin marketplace, helped thousands in Africa access global trade and finance tools. In Nigeria, Kenya, and Ghana, entrepreneurs used the platform to buy goods, pay freelancers, and hedge against local currency devaluation — all without needing a traditional bank.

A Freedom Tool in Ukraine

Amid the 2022 Ukraine crisis, crypto played a major humanitarian role. The Ukrainian government and NGOs raised over $100 million in crypto donations globally within weeks — funds used to support defense, food, and medical aid. Bitcoin, Ethereum, and even NFTs became financial lifelines in real time.

From Unbanked to Empowered – The El Salvador Experiment

El Salvador made history by becoming the **first country to adopt Bitcoin as legal tender**. Through apps like **Chivo Wallet**, many previously unbanked citizens could now send and receive money instantly. Bitcoin ATMs and educational programs were rolled out to help locals gain financial independence.

NFT Artists Changing Lives

Digital artists like **Beeple** (Mike Winkelmann), who sold an NFT artwork for $69 million, and **FEWOCiOUS**, a transgender teen who earned millions in NFT sales, found crypto as a platform to monetize creativity globally without middlemen.

Refugee Access to Assets with Bitcoin

For displaced individuals and refugees, carrying wealth in Bitcoin means escaping warzones or political oppression with financial sovereignty. Stories emerged from Afghanistan and Syria of families fleeing with their Bitcoin wallets — a silent revolution in asset protection.

Notes

This book draws on a wide range of research, case studies, and expert analyses to explore the transformative impact of cryptocurrency globally. Below are key sources and contextual notes supporting the book's main themes:

Environmental Impact of Cryptocurrency

UN Study on Bitcoin's Environmental Consequences:
Research by United Nations scientists highlights the significant environmental effects of cryptocurrency mining, including impacts on climate, water, and land. The study underscores the need for regulatory oversight and investment in more energy-efficient digital currencies, while also raising concerns about the inequitable distribution of benefits and harms across nations and generations.

Societal and Economic Impact

Academic Analysis of Crypto's Societal Role:
David Lucas Faria's dissertation reviews how cryptocurrencies, emerging after the 2008 financial crisis, have grown in importance due to their independence from central authorities. The work emphasizes the need for both business adoption and consumer awareness to fully realize crypto's potential to improve quality of life.

Digital Financial Inclusion via Blockchain:
A study published in *Frontiers in Blockchain* examines how blockchain technology has enabled greater financial inclusion, particularly for underserved populations. The research details blockchain's ability to lower transaction costs, facilitate remittances, enable crowdfunding, and expand access to credit and insurance, all of which are critical for sustainable development and poverty reduction.

Crypto for Social Good and Inclusion

Blockchain for Social Good:
Research in *SAGE Journals* analyzes narratives around using blockchain to promote social equity, privacy, and transparency. Case studies such as GrowBit illustrate how blockchain and cryptocurrency can incentivize education, teamwork, and collective action, while also highlighting the need to address deeper social and cultural inequalities for true inclusion.

Regulation, Risk, and Market Dynamics

Market Reactions to Regulation:
A 2024 SSRN paper investigates how different types of cryptocurrency regulation affect market risk and returns. The findings show that robust regulatory enforcement amplifies the intended effects of regulation, especially in liquid markets, and that cultural factors can influence regulatory outcomes.

Crypto Wealth and Real-World Economic Effects

Household Consumption and Crypto Wealth:
Transaction-level data from millions of U.S. households reveal that changes in crypto wealth can significantly impact household consumption and spill over into other asset classes, even though most users hold relatively small amounts of cryptocurrency.

Cultural and Social Narratives

The Online Culture of the Crypto Economy:
Ethnographic research explores the libertarian and anarcho-capitalist narratives prevalent in crypto communities. The study discusses how cryptocurrencies serve as both a critique of traditional financial systems and a tool for social resistance, enabling borderless, affordable, and instantaneous value transfer and remittances.

Additional Context

Financial Inclusion and Decentralized Finance:
Multiple studies referenced in this book emphasize that decentralized finance (DeFi) and blockchain-based solutions have the potential to democratize access to financial services, reduce costs, and foster innovation, especially in developing economies.

Risks and Challenges:
While the promise of cryptocurrency is substantial, the research also highlights challenges such as volatility, regulatory uncertainty, environmental impact, and the need for responsible participation and education.

These sources provide a foundation for understanding both the opportunities and complexities of cryptocurrency's role in transforming lives globally. For further reading and in-depth analysis, refer to the bibliography and recommended resources in the appendices.

www.ingramcontent.com/pod-product-compliance
Lightning Source LLC
Chambersburg PA
CBHW061216240926
51846CB00006B/1249